THE SECRET OF ADAPTABLE ORGANIZATION

HOW CAN YOU IMPROVE CULTURE, INNOVATION, PROMOTE MORALE, INSPIRE TRUST, AND KEEP NEGATIVITY AT BAY BY CREATING AN ADAPTABLE ORGANIZATION?

DR. AMIT DAS

To

All my bosses who made a difference in my professional career.

"Once Confucius said
As the water shapes
Itself to the vessel
That contains it,
So a wise man adapts
Himself to the circumstances.

Blaming the circumstances
Or people in the surrounding
For own misfortune or misery
Seldom yield tangible results
Instead a positive mindset
Faith, hope and courage
With willingness to adapt
Brings miraculous outcomes even in
The most adverse circumstances."

-Anonymous

Contents

Foreword

" The measure of intelligence is the ability to change."- Albert Einstein

Dear Readers,

Thank you for taking the time to learn more about the secrets of adaptive organization . The author recognizes that intelligent, motivated individuals like you have special gifts to give the world, but it's difficult to do in this VUCA business environment. The author has spent his entire professional career assisting managers in increasing their productivity, which he describes as the capacity to make progress on the results that matter most to them. professionally and individually. This book aims to teach you how critical it is to be adaptive every day toward achieving the things that matter most to you, leaving no stone unturned, and to develop a mindset of seeing the most overlooked aspects of life not only for what they are or appear to be, but also for what they could be. Through his profession, he's seen that the vast majority of time management advice offered doesn't help you enhance your life. This book outlines the importance of adaptive leadership, clearing your head of clutter, and sticking to a single-point agenda. The days of traditional, stability-oriented organizations are numbered. Organizations built for both stability and dynamism with networks of teams and people-centered cultures governed by common goals and co-created value for all stakeholders are replacing them. The Business Dictionary defines *"The Secret Of Adaptable Organization"* as a *"chameleon-like organization"* capable of keeping up with fast changes in its environment.

Regardless of the audience or venue, reading this book puts the reader on a unique and advantageous platform to connect in a more intelligent and successful manner. This book is well-researched and educational for people of all ages and genders. *"The Secret Of Adaptable Organization,"* this book is a quest to perceive even the most mundane things in a new light. Its goal is to assist you to harness your capacity to become more adaptive and use it to your advantage in order to rise above the mediocre tides in all aspects of your life. It reveals numerous methods for intentionally cultivating a mindset that refuses to be superficial about life.

To survive and prosper, an organization must be able to foresee, plan for, respond to, and adapt to problems and opportunities. It goes beyond risk management to take a more comprehensive view of a company's health and performance. An *"adaptive"* organization is one that not only survives, but also flourishes in the long run, surviving the test of time. Every company relies on its leadership to strengthen, organize, and shift resources in order to make the most efficient and effective use of them in order to enhance returns on investment and develop adaptiveness. Dr. Amit Das provides a step-by-step approach in this book on how to create an excellent adaptive culture at your firm. The author demonstrates how to uncover your hidden culture, transform ideals into actions, and open up communication across layers. To keep your culture thriving for the long term, the author emphasizes the significance of being clear from the top, building trust, and providing support structures. As Dr. Amit Das demonstrates in his book, by building your culture, you can increase communication, raise morale, encourage trust, and keep negativity at bay within your team. The author provides businesses with a step-by-step strategy for analysing, creating, and implementing iterative adaptive cultural transformation, with each success building on prior achievements. As a result, the company continues to adapt in ways that reduce stress, encourage learning, and promote organizational wellness.

Indeed, it may have increased as businesses realize their present systems are incapable of keeping up with the current rate of change. Transformation is not without danger, but adopting agility may mitigate this by giving organizations the resilience they need to deal with constant change. Consider whether your processes are flexible enough. Could your essential business systems adapt quickly to significant operational changes? Organizations with inbuilt adaptability skills are more likely than others to have responded quickly to the recent epidemic. Dr. Amit Das has interviewed hundreds of the most prolific performers to learn the best strategies for pursuing and maintaining organizational greatness. He discovered a pattern of unusual actions that distinguished these exceptional people. The book *"The Secret Of Adaptable Organization"* delves into how and where these efforts must be made in order for this to happen. The book is the result of the author's own endeavor to improve organizational performance. The most current concepts, as well as new observations and opinions, have been chosen and assembled. It will be extremely beneficial to the readers in their pursuit of perfection.

During these times of upheaval and uncertainty, many companies recognize the need for speed. Leaders perceive an opportunity to accelerate their firms' pace by doing even more in the areas mentioned above in the future. Respondents most typically cite more efficient decision making, clearer communication, and the use of technology to better engage consumers and staff when asked about the key chances to attain higher speed.The author offers the most effective tactics and step-by-step instructions for you to construct your own particular road to excellence in this book. You'll also find better methods to collaborate with colleagues, respond more effectively to coaching and mentoring, and become more positive and self-directed in your thoughts and actions, resulting in more personal and professional pleasure. This book attempts to provide insights into the many pathways, courses, and drives that world-class enterprises have constructed in order to achieve the pinnacles of greatness. This book provides cutting-edge material, including innovative and unusual study aids as well as fresh, thought-provoking content, with an emphasis on integrating corporate agility, or adaptiveness, into practical management.

There is no exact formula for predicting the future of any industry; nonetheless, business executives can envision the next day based on the unique qualities of each organization. What is the present cash flow situation, and how will it evolve in the future?

Are the products or services available to customers beneficial both during and after the crisis? If not, what are your options? Organizations do not adapt quickly enough to keep up with changing requirements, and governance and management methods do not generate the required results. Ineffective communication exacerbates these issues. The development of a good organizational performance system can help to solve these issues. The contents of this book will provide a deep reservoir of ideas and techniques for producing remarkable outcomes, competitive advantages, and long-term results for leaders, consultants, and organizational advisors. The book *"The Secret Of Adaptable Organization"* draws on first-hand experience from high-performance operations to deliver vital adaptive leadership lessons as well as clear, accessible, and practical insights on managing teams in any corporate setting. This book provides a new and fascinating viewpoint on the factors that influence team and organizational greatness. Dr. Amit Das, the book's author, has a unique combination of expertise and insight, having worked as a management consultant. His insights and interviews from business sectors are used to demonstrate the obstacles to high performance and leadership.

The materials include a performance model that can be applied to a wide range of organizations, focusing on people's attitudes rather than skills; a process for closing the gap between desired and actual outcomes; how to accelerate performance in real time; exhibiting a set of behaviours that the capacity of an organization to function efficiently, adapt properly, adjust correctly, and grow from within is referred to as organizational health. The author also looks at whether great leaders are born or made, how lean ideas are used differently in various organizations, and why clever individuals fail so often after being promoted to management positions. Take a path that leads to significant performance increases and a great culture where everyone is prepared to succeed with this leadership.

Just like strategy, writing a book takes deep contemplation to narrate a theory in a very lucid manner. Hence, the author could establish his thought process for readers.

So, happy reading and learning to all readers.
Carpe diem.
Dr. Amit Das

Preface

It's Not A Secret Anymore

"The reasonable man adapts himself to the world; the unreasonable one persists in trying to adapt the world to himself. Therefore all progress depends on the unreasonable man." -George Bernard Shaw

In business, change is the only constant, although it is rarely as unexpected or as overpowering as it has been in 2022. The coronavirus pandemic has upended a number of industries, from hospitality to energy, that appeared positioned for success in the new decade until lately. Businesses are now scrambling to pick up the debris while navigating an uncertain future. Under normal conditions, change management is a difficult task. However, when COVID-19 is taken into account, organizational transformation takes on a whole new meaning. Your life may improve by accident, but your initiatives will not. With author , you can start managing your organization more effectively. What exactly is adaptability? Being adaptable means being flexible. Accepting change is the definition of adaptability. Adaptability is the practice of fine-tuning methods. While agility or adaptability has always been crucial in the modern workplace, it is now more important than ever. In this unique situation, businesses that adapt quickly and establish a new normal are more likely to prosper.

Why Chameleons?

Chameleons are wonderful animals. They have been around for almost 100 million years. Chameleons change color to blend in with their environment or to stand out from predators and other chameleons. Their eyes can stare in opposing directions at the same time, which helps them see predators and food. They can predict and adapt to a wide range of settings, including hostile and rapidly changing ecosystems like rainforests and deserts. Unlike other animals, such as dodos or dinosaurs, which became extinct when their habitat changed dramatically, they have demonstrated the capacity to not only adapt and survive, but also thrive. To put it another way, these species are actually adaptable. Being adaptive does not imply that you are unaware of your identity. Chameleons only change color when they need to. If they're on a leaf, they're green if they should be, and if they're on a branch, they're brown if they should be. It understands what hue to show when it isn't near anything it needs to adjust to. The chameleon was aware of his own nature and content with who he was. It is quite similar for an organization to be adaptable as well . Organizations, like chameleons, are aware of what they are, their values, and their skills. However, it understands the need to adjust to changes in their surroundings. Organizations have evolved in the era of knowledge and information, and they've become more interested in finding ways to survive that allow them to keep up with the environment and the next digital age, which will put them on the cusp of organizational wisdom. Organizations have entered the digital age, and they've had to adapt to changing circumstances and attitudes. There will be a need for the chameleon organization to alter in response to the changing environment. As a result of the massive explosion in amazing technology and in all fields of environmental and other, this development has been leaping forward at a rapid pace, and it appears that their main concern is how to control competitors and clients. On the other hand, to be proactive rather than reactive, through the adoption of some of the dimensions that enable them to survive and grow in the digital age.

What happens if you put pressure on a crystal glass? It usually becomes weaker over time and finally breaks. Crystal glasses, like many other items and living things, are delicate. What is the polar opposite of delicate? Strong, tenacious, and adaptable come to mind. Being robust, resilient, and flexible, on the other hand, is not the polar opposite of being fragile. It is *"adaptable" or "agile."* When you push on it, it not only bounces back but it bounces harder. It's almost as if it's a muscle. It expands as you stretch it or apply power to it. Larger, more established organizations can also be adaptable. *"Adapt or die,"* the song says; death is a bit dramatic, but it's about being able to adjust to rapid changes faster than your competitors. The fact is clear: some businesses will position themselves to swiftly adapt to the ever-increasing rate of change, while others will become obsolete and finally cease to exist. While the likelihood of businesses dying has grown with time, the true picture of the impact of rapid change on organizations is more complex. If companies want to know how to effectively respond to these issues, they must not only think about the correct change management theories, procedures, and strategies, but they must also think about mindset and behavior transformation, since that is the true difficulty.

Organizations that learn and adapt to problems in a volatile, unpredictable, complex, and ambiguous (VUCA) business environment have a significant competitive edge. Leaders must adjust as well, frequently making significant changes because their roles might be procedural and rule-driven. The author of "" explains how to apply systems thinking to any framework in order to become more adaptable and effective in a rapidly changing world. Anyone who runs an organization or an organizational endeavor will tell you that things are changing quickly and that the difficulties you all face are becoming more complicated. The acronym VUCA, which stands for Volatile, Uncertain, Complex, and Ambiguous, was invented by the military. This applies equally to the private and governmental sectors as it does to any other. Leaders must be adaptable and sensitive to the fast-changing world in order to flourish in this VUCA environment. This begins with paying attention to critical input that will lead you to the result you aim to achieve via your organizational efforts. It is your responsibility as a systems leader to build an organization that can adapt to the difficulties it confronts on a daily basis. In this book *"The Secret Of Adaptable Organization"*, the author will discuss how you may become a leader who thoroughly knows how you think, allowing your team to tackle any problem, issue, or scenario and turn insight into unique ideas for real effect and change. Systems thinking entails attempting to comprehend the systems that surround you. To do more than just respond to circumstances as they occur. Instead, consider how the world truly works. In today's fast-changing competitive VUCA world, merely pursuing efficiency would not be enough. So the author will show you a framework for establishing adaptable companies that are quick and agile in responding to market changes.

Your mission is to build an organization that learns how to adapt and survive. To do this, you must promote organizational learning aimed at increasing your capability to meet organizational goals. Leaders must also realize that organizational results are not something that can be generated directly, but rather indirectly, through instilling a set of simple norms that govern each group member's work. To develop system-level behavior, you must concentrate on the underlying rules that generate it. The issue is that CEOs, administrators, and other organizational leaders are always striving to get more out of their teams and organizations in order to improve both internal efficiency and outward influence. They want to work smarter and leave a bigger impression on the world faster. The issue is that humans do not act like a collection of gears. Their intentions are often mixed, and you're all aware that they may participate in more subtle types of resistance, which gears do not.

You don't get to choose whether or not your organization is a complex adaptive system since it is made up of individuals interacting socially and with their surroundings. However, you have the option of embracing this reality and using it to your benefit. All companies have the potential to be learning organizations. This is due to their capability to gather and respond to input from the real world, such as consumer data, market forces, and competition. The majority of organizational challenges you confront are caused by gaps between how organizations actually operate and how you believe they work. As a result of feedback, these things get more aligned. It is the leader's responsibility to foster a culture that values and changes in response to input.Failure must be considered a chance to learn.To compete, people must be encouraged to try and retest their ideas, as well as given room to iterate. This is adaptation, and adaptable organizations are the result of adaptive leadership.

Are you a leader who can adapt?

Because the world is changing at a breakneck pace, leaders come in a variety of sizes and forms. If you've been keeping up with the newest leadership trends, you've definitely already heard about several techniques and ideals that have proven successful for many current and prospective business leaders. To be honest, there is no right or wrong way to lead, as long as you have the best interests of your team and your company at heart. But what if your squad isn't going to stay the same for long? It will shift. And it's not only your team that will alter; it's your workplace culture, your market, everything. This is when you put one of your essential leadership characteristics, namely adaptability, to the test. In this piece, author'll offer some statistics on why and how adaptability is a critical component of leadership, regardless of the team or organization with which you're working. In addition, you'll discover some of my finest ideas and methods for being an adaptive leader in a fast-paced sector. Most significantly, flexibility is changing to suit new conditions and obstacles, which will ensure your company's or organization's success. Why is it vital for a leader to be adaptable? Change is unavoidable. Everything grows and evolves into something better, including the workplace dynamic, corporate strategy, and technological advancements. Adapting and responding is the only way to survive as a leader and face the complexity of change, whether you like it or not.

Everything is available at the press of a button in today's competitive world, and life is fast and seamless, with an internet highway running parallel to us. Connecting via virtual setup has become a necessary element of our lives. This, paired with the impending danger of COVID-19, has made working from home and on internet platforms the new normal. The hybrid office is more popular than ever. A hybrid workplace is one in which some workers work from the office while others work from home. This gives you greater control over when and where you finish your job. Whether or not there is a pandemic, several large corporations are adopting permanent remote employment now. Even after COVID, companies like Google have stated that they will continue to use hybrid mode. Similar moves have been contemplated by several other corporations, including Microsoft, Twitter, and Verizon. Unfortunately, employees in India are struggling to cope with the heavy demand. Burnout among employees is on the rise. Employee happiness and productivity are inextricably linked. Many corporate executives were terrified of flexible work environments before the COVID-19 epidemic. Just a few weeks ago, the prospect of all workers working from home for weeks or months would have prompted panic attacks. You do know, however, that achieving this *"new normal"* would require significant transformation inside our businesses and organizations. There will be extra challenges for teams to be able to problem solve effectively, develop strong solutions and execute them across the business and activities in a timely and efficient fashion.

Acknowledgements

At the outset I will thank to my family for supporting me throughout the journey of writing my book and encouraging me to live my dreams- my son has always been instrumental in giving his inspiration to complete the writing of this book. Despite the fact that I am listed as the author of this book, "The Secret Of Adaptable Organization" would not have been published if I had depended entirely on my own talents. To create this book required more than a village—it took a family of dedicated and caring people who were always prepared to lend a hand.

Writing a book while working full-time is no simple task, so I'd want to express my gratitude to my amazing coworkers, who act as mentors and cheerleaders in equal measure. Thank you, too, to the rest of the accumentor team for your patience and unflinching support while I worked on this book!

Thank you to everyone who has listened to me argue for doing everything you can to make your life, including your work life, more progressive. I appreciate everyone's assistance throughout the process. This book would not have been possible without each of you having had an impact on my life in some manner.

Lastly, I would like to thank all the people whom I have been associated, you gave me power. I would like to thank Notion Press for publishing my book. At last thank you all for gifting your time to read out this book.

I'd want to convey my heartfelt appreciation to the Almighty God for bestowing his blessings and being so gracious.

INTRODUCTION

Adopting An Ecosystem Mindset

"It is not the strongest of the species that survives, nor the most intelligent. It is the one that is most adaptable to change. "
- Charles Darwin

In today's business environment, organizations that see themselves as part of an ecosystem compete better. They have more visibility into their consumers' demands and behaviors when they use external communities, partnerships, and alliances. Adaptable organizations are able to identify changes in the external environment rapidly and adapt accordingly. Adaptive work frequently entails challenging an organization's underlying assumptions, challenging the status quo, and implementing changes that may appear harsh but are required. Adaptive capacity refers to a person's ability to cope with change and challenges to the status quo. It also includes how a person responds to situational circumstances with suitable actions rather than default inclinations and behaviors. When company executives recognize that the circumstances are in charge, they may choose actions that boost their adaptability. As a result, leadership becomes more adaptable. Because the future is fundamentally unpredictable, adaptable leadership is essential for long-term success. COVID- Leaders who could adjust to unpredictability were differentiated from those who couldn't.

The world you've known has altered dramatically in only a few years. But, despite this trying moment, keep in mind that generations before you suffered similar difficulties. Your forefathers and mothers, like you, were strong, kind, and determined. The COVID-19 outbreak was quite transitory. You've come out the other side stronger and wiser. Covid-19 has caused widespread alarm for companies and communities all around the world, unlike anything you've ever seen before. The epidemic has brought attention to the need for businesses to be adaptive, but business executives have long recognized this requirement. They had to deal with various problems even before the chaos of 2020. Most corporate executives believe they have been in a perpetual state of *"transformation"* for the past two decades, and many are weary of hearing the phrase. It is still doing so. Many industries have been affected. Leaders must set their own interests aside in any tough scenario and devote their resources and efforts to the greater good. True leaders are visionaries. They are visionaries who encourage creativity and innovation. They provide comfort.

The COVID-19 issue compelled enterprises all around the world to rethink many elements of their jobs, workforce, and workplace, while also introducing new dangers and opportunities. New business start-ups nearly quadrupled from pre-pandemic levels. Larger companies also went through an *"unfreezing"* period in which the status quo of how things were done was challenged. In these exceptional times, businesses have faced unexpected problems and have been attempting to adapt to new methods of working. While businesses strive to minimize the impact on their operations, it is unavoidable that the pandemic has influenced many businesses' future organizational management strategies. The pandemic has heightened the trend of employers taking a greater interest in their employees' financial, physical, and mental health. Some organizations helped the community by moving operations to produce items or provide services to aid in the fight against the epidemic, as well as donating community relief funds and free community services.

The epidemic not only interrupted people's lives, but it also provided an opportunity for companies to rethink who they are and where they want to go. Organizations must take advantage of this potential to turn uncertainty into opportunity throughout their work, workforce, and workplace. Organizations should close the loop by supporting their workers' needs after redesigning the job to be done and putting people first. Employers must have a clear vision for their working paradigm, whether hybrid, in-person, or remote. However, clarity alone isn't enough. Employees want greater freedom after a live remote work experience, and many will need a good reason to return to in-person work. Organizations that solve these issues get a better employee experience, higher loyalty, and more access to talent pools. The new workplace, in whatever shape it takes, has the potential to bring out the best in people by giving them what they want. As a result, higher productivity and customer satisfaction are realized. Employee expectations as a result of the epidemic suggest that businesses reassess their work processes. From the C-suite to the shop floor, employees want more meaning in their jobs.

Businesses that have specific agreements and action plans and work autonomously to attain their goals. The action instructions were co-created and disseminated by one or more people, who were accidentally amplified as a consequence of the good outcome, which, depending on the circumstances, expanded their reach. Some organizations have already done so and gone even farther (Amazon, Google, Netflix, Airbnb, WeWork, Facebook, LinkedIn, Kanbanzone, Zoom), while others are in the process. There are many success stories in Mexico, but more are required. The outcomes, as well as the effort, arise from the iterative, incremental, and emergent execution.

As you've seen, organizations are always confronted with technological and adaptive obstacles. Adaptive challenges provide a more unclear problem to be solved, whereas technical challenges have a well defined problem that can be solved by professionals. Adaptive leadership as a framework can be a beneficial method to handle such issues. Furthermore, despite the hurdles that come with this strategy, building this skill allows businesses to prosper in the long run.

When an organism adapts in nature, it builds on its previous capabilities while generating completely new functionality. In evolution, God did not use a zero-based budgeting system. You pay homage to the past while also determining what you can let go of for the sake of adaptability. For those who are losing, the losses are severe. The adaptable Organization is a fundamental shift in operating and management philosophy that allows large-scale global businesses to think like startups and drive current people practices that enable enterprise agility through empowered networks of teams. The Environment In the past, in more stable times, companies gained a competitive edge by making gradual efforts to become more standardized, efficient, and better at doing what they'd been doing for a long time. Organizational survival in uncertain times necessitates the knowledge that companies are part of a larger external ecosystem, bound together by a distinct, customer-centric purpose that is continually developing to remain relevant. You can learn the following from clients who are adopting an ecosystem mindset:

- A common purpose is the glue that holds an ecosystem together, despite ongoing iteration and adaptation. It considers the organization's success from the perspectives of consumers, stakeholders, and society. As a result, people who are engaged in meaningful work are more likely to achieve the company's goals.
- Businesses and organizations will eventually have to conduct their operations on a different playing field, with different rules and, in many cases, fewer teams. Employee safety must come first, with social isolation measures and remote working possibilities the most urgent problems to address and overcome.
- Using customer-focused missions, a bold corporate purpose cascades across the business. Teams work efficiently on their individual tasks without interfering with one another, but they

are held together by a long-term organizational commitment.

- In these incredibly trying times, investing in and harmonizing your CI (Continuous Improvement) efforts today might prove to be a critical move in helping you achieve a competitive edge and maximize your company's performance for tomorrow.

- Basic concepts for self-organization include decentralization of decision-making; flattening of traditional hierarchies; role changes; and the formation of agile teams, all of which imply rapid and expedient decision-making. These fundamental principles are put into practice to enable a manner of doing and concreting things; they also stem from values, which shape a style of thinking and provide higher work plan sustainability.

- Embracing change, having a flexible attitude, actionable thinking, learning from prior experiences, and having agile values and principles may all help us boost your chances of surviving a crisis.

- Organizations learn because they are complex, adaptive systems made up of individuals. This type of learning must be the foundation of any business. While the organization's vision is the ultimate aim that drives it, the vision, as well as the organization's capacity and mission, should constantly and continually be informed by learning. Organizational learning is the source of new capabilities and the driving force behind adaptable organizations. Because organizational learning happens all the time, adaptive leaders must create a culture in which organizational members are acutely aware of this fundamental, continuing function.

- A self-organizing system forms an ordered structure based on certain suitable principles as it advances. The better a company's capacity to identify, produce, and operate new talents to efficiently adapt to its environment, the stronger its self-organization is.

- Flexible governance frameworks are required to support an Adaptable Organization. When bureaucracy is reduced, choices are clear, and individuals are empowered, governance allows for adaptive work. It is recommended to use a test-and-learn strategy to implementation. Rather of a loud explosion, the path to becoming an adaptable organization is a succession of tiny, gradual improvements.

- In order to achieve the goal, there must be a unified emphasis on how to expand capabilities and optimise systems to enable your business to perform its job faster, cheaper, and better.
- Given how long most organizations take to make a choice and then act on it, this was an urgent need for more agility on short notice. Employee requirements, consumer expectations, and economic instability are all areas where agility is emphasized – and will continue to be.
- A leadership team may select where to focus their attention, plan, and establish a stronger organizational resilience state in the future through a comprehensive evaluation.
- Teams execute in an iterative and empowered manner. Teams must embrace an agile, *"fail fast"* mindset that allows them to adapt quickly to changing client expectations through regular touchpoints, iteration reviews, and cross-team planning. Only when decision-making powers are transparent and teams are allowed freedom and autonomy is this achievable.
- Agile transformations require enthusiastic believers to help them succeed. The supporters should be well-informed and experienced practitioners who can attest to the benefits. They will aid in the development of grassroots support for the change.
- Capability development refers to the ability to create, perform, or deploy resources toward a certain purpose. Organizations, like people, have numerous sorts of capacity. What you see is what you see with your eyes. What you do is your mission. And capacity is a level of preparedness that enables you to carry out your objective. It's a system within a system. Adaptable organizations must manage customer adaptation and scalable efficiency at the same time. They acknowledge the importance of both and strike a good balance by combining functional and cross-functional, centralized and decentralized teams.

- Adaptable organizations place a higher focus on the team and use team composition and new ways of working to unleash individual potential. In an adaptable organization, good team growth looks like this: The realization that team composition is inextricably tied to individual performance. Individuals can only fully prosper when their different viewpoints, distinct skillsets, and wide experience are brought together. a distinct focus that brings the team together around the organization's mission.

- Adaptive workplaces, a more fluid model that gives workers more freedom to work from wherever they are most productive, allowing them to do their best job and produce better results for employers, will likely be the way of the future.

- Organizations that prioritize employee engagement perceive increased productivity as well as other advantages such as decreased turnover and more innovation. Organizations with low engagement, on the other hand, have poorer productivity, more turnover, and higher degrees of burnout.

- Adaptive workspaces provide the best of both worlds in terms of increasing productivity. While government agencies are still adjusting to the fast virtualization of work, new research shows that firms that use adaptable workplaces reap considerable organizational and labor benefits.

- Finally, organizational learning through feedback expands capability. Aside from that, capability must be quantifiable. This means that you must finally develop some metric for determining how effective your capacity is in terms of mission enablement.Because capability is a natural function of an organization, the purpose of leadership is to steer it toward an enabling mission, which leads to vision.

The existence of pressure and tremendous obstacles is a constant for business systems in today's times, as is the standard in business. As a result of technology's immediacy and face-to-face engagement with other latitudes, you may live internationally, but you also increase your vulnerability to hazards that were formerly global but now produce turbulence in your own environs. A worldwide crisis can increase the uncertainty and volatility in business transactions as well as in a country's economic, social, and political situation. It has direct or indirect repercussions on businesses, depending on the reason. Any unintentional, natural, or intentional event that has the potential to have a significant impact on business, people, the environment, or the local and global community as a natural or human-instigated fact that disrupts the normal operation of business systems is referred to as a crisis. To make a breakthrough from the way you thought and acted, you should probably change your way of thinking, unlearning, and relearning; the change is not implemented only with thought, with desire; it is necessary to take action; if this action leads us to manage your company in a completely different, self-organized manner, you are preparing yourselves for almost everything. Remember that the Japanese word for crisis is *"opportunity for progress."* Negative changes in returns, decreasing job morale, and declining incomes are all signs of a crisis.

The stable organizational structures may encourage order, unambiguous decision-making, and functional silos to ensure optimal efficiency when change is predictable. Traditional organizational frameworks, on the other hand, cannot keep up in an era of exponential change. What you're starting to see in terms of adaptable organization structure and design: Both official and informal institutions must be aligned with customer-focused goals. Traditional techniques frequently compel organizations to work in a strictly functional or matrix context without considering the impact on human networks.

Effective organizational leadership necessitates leaders and team members quickly focusing on executing the organization's purpose in order to realise its vision with maximum efficiency and success. This starts with a clear, quantifiable, and attainable vision. The most succinct definition of vision is a desired future objective or condition, but a good vision must also possess a variety of additional characteristics. But first, let us explain why a vision should be a future aim or condition. Every organization tends to progress toward a state. What differs is whether the movement is concerted, directed, and coordinated, and whether it represents a desired future condition. The present economic crisis has also stretched the boundaries of how corporations perceive employee satisfaction. Employing such measures can be an effective way to improve employees' physical health and emotional well-being. While some firms recognized the pandemic's humanitarian catastrophe and emphasized employees' well-being as people over employees' well-being as workers, others have forced employees to work in high-risk environments with no assistance, considering them as workers first and people second.

Summing Up

Adaptable organizations are able to identify changes in the external environment rapidly and adapt accordingly. Adaptive work frequently entails challenging an organization's underlying assumptions, challenging the status quo, and implementing changes that may appear harsh but are required. Leaders must set their own interests aside in any tough scenario and devote their resources and efforts to the greater good. Organizations that solve these issues get a better employee experience, higher loyalty, and more access to talent pools. The new workplace, in whatever shape it takes, has the potential to bring out the best in people by giving them what they want. The Adaptable Organization is a fundamental shift in operating and management philosophy that allows large-scale global businesses to think like startups. Adaptable leaders must create a culture in which organizational members are acutely aware of this fundamental, continuing function. In an adaptable organization, good team growth looks like this: The realization that team composition is inextricably tied to individual performance.

CHAPTER TWO

ROADBLOCKS & CHALLENGES

Building A Resilient Organization In A Chaotic And Complex World

"The most successful people are those who accept and adapt to constant change. This adaptability requires a degree of flexibility and humility most people can't manage." —Paul Lutus

COVID-19 has given businesses a new reality. It has prompted a significant paradigm shift, forcing companies to prepare for the future and embrace a people-first approach to the current problem. The escalating COVID-19 socioeconomic catastrophe is compelling business executives throughout the world to react quickly to the epidemic and its repercussions on their companies. The coronavirus illness of 2019-20 has caught the globe off guard and has had a significant impact on many people's lives, especially those in the business sector and its stakeholders. Thousands of businesses have developed crisis management strategies, with many of them moving to a completely virtual workplace. Businesses have faced several obstacles as a result of the COVID-19 situation. Many businesses have already suffered financial losses, and the World Economic Forum estimates that the global economy will be affected by $1 trillion. Employers are becoming more nimble in order to tackle these challenges. Companies made significant efforts to protect employees as the COVID-19 outbreak turned into a pandemic on short notice.

While the benefits of being an adaptable organization are obvious, conventional businesses will encounter difficulties in making the move. Moving from hierarchical to servant leadership, as well as devolving governance and decision-making to teams at the customer-facing level, poses difficulties for traditional leadership paradigms. It will be difficult for an organization to maintain a flexible mentality and culture digitally if the modular digital infrastructure can not match rising demand. Creating an agile work culture that values and supports cross-team cooperation, ownership of outcomes, and information flow necessitates various behaviors, attitudes, and abilities, which can be difficult for bigger, more complicated organizations. To be effective, any enterprise-wide transformation would require constant executive support and direction. A big bang approach to change, on the other hand, may be difficult in a risk-averse company climate that requires validation of success within each management cycle. Another option is to use adaptive principles to improve a specific customer-facing function. Within this business sector, new cross-functional and network-based teams aligned to particular client goals might be formed and established utilizing agile approaches. Simultaneously, via training and mentorship, assist the organization in adopting servant leadership abilities, structures, and practices. The purposeful application of leadership, governance, and decision-making with new agile teams, with proper feedback loops and escalation channels, is required.

To manage the crisis with resilience and ensure long-term business survival, successfully managing social distancing and making remote working possible has become critical. Concerns about employee engagement and productivity have obviously moved to the forefront. According to a recent LinkedIn survey, 95% of talent management professionals in India believe that employee experience is one of the most important factors influencing the future of employees and the organization as a whole. People analytics is a difficulty for 55% of HR directors, according to the same survey. In order to audit and analyze organizational and employee productivity, HR analytics (to make data-driven choices) has become even more vital in this new world. Gone are the days when HR's duty was confined to filling vacancies as and when they arose. The role of human resources in today's business environment is more important than ever.

The moment has arrived for a more comprehensive view of flexibility. Embracing the where, when, and how of flexibility will give you a competitive edge in recruiting fresh talent. The financial argument is clear: provide genuine freedom to keep and develop your workforce—or watch your employees go. Organizations must also find methods to reset expectations of 24/7 availability and avoid enforcing inflexible hours on employees in order to retain staff. Organizations must have faith that the task will be completed and that workers will have enough time and energy to attend to their personal obligations and well-being. Email blackout periods were established by one big automotive business, with employees' capacity to send and receive work emails being disabled on weekends and corporate holidays.

According to the survey, employers in India are substantially more amenable to recruiting remote workers than in other Asia-Pacific nations. HR should take on a larger role. Employees in India faced lengthy shifts when working remotely, and attrition climbed 1.5 times by 2020. According to the research, HR will now play a major role in helping enterprises simplify their operations, create their strategy, and hire more effectively, even beyond COVID-19, as hints of a second wave intensify India's remote working demands. As remote work grows more common, HR experts are increasingly advising employers to prioritize employee engagement. It's past time for businesses to rethink their approach to flexibility. Whether it's work-life balance, physical and mental wellness, or family care, today's employees need flexibility suited to their unique requirements. As they collaborate with HR to build unique, innovative solutions for their direct reports, managers will play a crucial role in personalizing flexibility for their direct reports.

Many firms had developed their value propositions and educated their sales personnel on how to sell before the COVID-19 epidemic. Many salespeople master the ability to persuade consumers that they need to buy now rather than later to remedy an issue. As a result of the COVID-19 pandemic, customers have gained the ability to resist the sales rep. The simple conclusion is that this worldwide epidemic affected all businesses and organizations, whether large or small, in some manner. The degree of influence will differ depending on the industry you work in and the exact product or service you provide. The great majority, on the other hand, will be constrained in their capacity to sell their products or services and will be under growing pressure to cut costs.

The post-COVID period is characterized by turmoil and volatility in the commercial world. You have seen over the last 10 years, in the pre-COVID period, that a learning organization is a major differentiator from its competitors and creates a more lively, customer-responsive culture. However, in the post-COVID age, more is required. It has already been noticed that having a learning organization is not enough to obtain a competitive advantage; employees must also demonstrate adaptive performance. Organizations are continually looking for individuals who can learn and adapt to the changing needs of the business world. As a result of technological advancements and organizational reorganization, employees must learn new skills and improve their flexibility. Organizations must perform well in these area of adaptive performance for organizations to obtain competitive advantages in the post-COVID future.

Be thoughtful in your approach and consider the long-term consequences of employee experience. If remote and on-site personnel have been treated differently, address the disparities. Engage task employees in a team culture and foster an inclusive environment. Organizations were already confronting greater employee expectations for openness prior to COVID-19. Staff and potential applicants will evaluate companies based on how they handled employees throughout the epidemic. Balance today's efforts to address acute pandemic concerns with the long-term impact on the employment brand. Assist CEOs and executive leaders in making judgments on executive pay cutbacks, for example, and ensure that the financial consequences are borne by executives rather than the entire workforce. Progressive companies communicate freely and regularly to demonstrate how they support their staff despite cost-cutting efforts. Look for ways to form talent-sharing relationships with other firms to help employees who have been displaced by COVID-19 find new employment. According to a 2019 Gartner organization design study, 55% of organizational redesigns focused on simplifying roles, supply chains, and procedures in order to improve efficiency. While this method captured efficiency, it also introduced vulnerabilities since systems are unable to adapt to interruptions.

The existing order has been upended by the COVID-19 epidemic, environmental concerns, and societal unrest. Organizations in all industries are being forced to change at a faster rate than ever before. Even major incumbent organizations have had to adjust to the world's largest agile working experiment during the last year, showing that old dogs can learn new tricks. Organizations must now be able to adjust their operations and consumer offers with breakneck speed, yet outdated systems, processes, and approaches frequently stymie them. How can they better prepare themselves to respond better and faster—to become more flexible and prosper in the face of perpetual change? Organizations with shorter, more detailed planning horizons can repeatedly reprioritise efforts based on current needs. Leaders must be willing to adjust goals and designs when company objectives shift and feedback from early iterations emerges. Agile product ownership and backlog management strategies might aid in this situation, especially when making potentially emotional decisions objectively.

While the COVID epidemic emphasizes the importance of agility and speed in the workplace, it's critical to remember that it's not about completing everything at breakneck speed. Looking for inventive methods to enhance company resilience, future-proof income sources, improve processes, and ensure staff are well-managed and supported is what organizational agility is all about. I find it intriguing that both the McKinsey and Workday studies found that organizations with integrated agile skills, such as data accessibility and cross-functional cooperation, were more likely than others to adapt quickly to the epidemic.

Leaders can not know whether or not their companies are actually resilient unless they are put to the test. In their 2021 Resilience Report, Deloitte highlighted five characteristics of resilient businesses, which business executives may mimic to create better resilience in their own organizations following a turbulent 2020. Most resilient firms prioritize all of these characteristics, not just one or two. This is partly due to the fact that these traits frequently overlap and complement one another. To nurture and sustain them, you'll need desire, effort, investment, and action. Most significantly, the evidence indicates that speed is key. During the COVID-19 crisis, organizations that made early investments in resilient strategies—or, even better, had previously made strategic, personnel, and technological investments in resilience-enhancing capabilities—outperformed their competitors. This study demonstrates a key lesson learned from the pandemic: resilience is as much about planning ahead as it is about responding to and recovering from a disaster.What five resilience attributes may companies use to succeed in the face of adversity? By deliberately nurturing these qualities, your company will be better positioned to overcome upheavals and bring in a new normal. Deloitte Global's fourth annual preparation study examines the topic of organizational resilience in the face of a turbulent 2020. You must be eager to hear how businesses are dealing with the unforeseen obstacles you experienced in the previous year, as well as your thoughts on what made your businesses more or less resilient to upheaval.

A secure environment for collaboration and linked working. This is accomplished through flexible communication, human connection, and alignment with the larger organization's objective. True collaboration can help organizations achieve more agility by unlocking latent productivity and inclusiveness.Creating flexible workplaces How can the public sector make use of COVID-19's lessons? The typical "office day" has evolved. After nearly a year of the world's tremendous overnight transition to a virtual work environment, the public sector's perspective on remote and virtual work has fundamentally shifted. People may do their work swiftly, effectively, and pleasantly while working remotely, thanks to this forced move toward a dispersed and highly virtualized work environment. It has demolished the myth that employees can't be as productive while they're working remotely.

Although research into the influence of COVID-19 on organizational structure, job design, and employee well-being has increased, few studies have looked into the importance of leadership and what it takes to be a successful leader under such circumstances. Using the COVID-19 crisis as a case study, this study combines social cognition theory and conservation of resources theory to argue for the role of adaptable personalities in the creation of competent leaders during times of crisis. You contend that managers with an adaptable personality have higher levels of self-efficacy for leading during a crisis, resulting in higher motivation to lead during the COVID-19 crisis. Furthermore, it is suggested that managers with increased motivation to lead during the COVID-19 crisis have improved adaptive performance, implying a serial mediation model in which crisis leader self-efficacy and motivation to lead during the COVID-19 crisis act as explanatory mechanisms of the relationship between the adaptive personality and the manager's performance. To test our hypothesis, the author gathered data from more than 100 full-time managers in India during the COVID-19 crisis and analyzed it using hierarchical linear regression. All of the hypotheses are supported by the findings. It includes a discussion of the findings, contributions, limits, and future directions. COVID-19 has had a significant impact on the globe in a variety of fields and businesses. Changes in the implementation of a country's education system are one of COVID-19's significant impacts. The school authorities had to cope with a variety of concerns and obstacles that arose as a result of the debate. Changes in the media and teaching techniques employed at the school level, as well as in other educational institutions, demonstrate this. To maintain the continuity of teaching and learning, school administrators should adopt a proactive approach. As a result, this study discusses adaptive leadership, resilience development, and leadership duty distribution.

In addition, this report discusses some novel culture-fostering methods for school leaders to use during the COVID-19 endemic phase. The findings suggest that school leaders should take action and influence the school atmosphere so that the school ecosystem can work together to address the situation. The concept of *"continuous improvement"* appears straightforward, but it needs a skilled leader to make it work. Many educational groups currently promote a *"continuous improvement"* strategy that appears easy and unassailable: define an issue, devise a solution, test it, see whether it works, change it as necessary, and continue the process indefinitely.

Making headway on difficult problems COVID-19, societal difficulties, and conflicts have all necessitated making quick modifications in the previous two years. Moving forward with these complex issues puts new strains on your abilities and encourages us to develop at the cutting edge of your abilities. You'll need new tools, frameworks, and solutions to do so. explains Accepting responsibility for assisting others in achieving a common goal in the face of adversity is key. The ability to remain calm in the face of adversity is crucial. That is why, in today's world, you require this style of leadership. Over the years, leadership has evolved from a technical process to a much more adaptable one, requiring figuring out how to assist people deal with uncertainty.

If the COVID-19 epidemic has taught us anything, it's that firms must be more adaptable. In order to respond to constant change, they must be able to pivot. Agility has become a catchphrase for doing things better, but it is also a commercial requirement. In difficult circumstances, I believe it is normal, even wise, to be cautious when considering new investments. When budgets are limited, the first lever that finance pulls is innovation. Nonetheless, the current scenario has not slowed many global organizations' progress toward digital transformation.

Businesses were forced to deal with unforeseen upheaval and devise solutions on the fly as a result of the epidemic. This adaptability will be critical to success in 2022. This post will explain what adaptive capability is, why it's vital, and how HR can assist leaders in embracing it. It's reasonable to assume that the epidemic threw the corporate world into disarray. Before the epidemic, the rate of change was extraordinary, but the pandemic drove it beyond normalcy. Not only did leaders have to foresee and implement their teams' success, but they also had to be adaptable in order to deal with the wide range of challenges that arose.

Resilient organizations are better equipped to adapt to change and correct course more swiftly. Design roles and structures around objectives to boost agility and flexibility, and define how processes might flex to create a more responsive company. It provides workers with a variety of positions that are adaptable and flexible so that they may gain cross-functional knowledge and training. Following the global financial crisis, global M&A activity increased, and many firms were nationalized to avoid disaster. As the epidemic fades, mergers and acquisitions (M & A) and company nationalization will accelerate. To minimize and manage risk in times of change, companies will focus on growing their geographic diversification and investing in secondary markets. As operating models change, the complexity of scale and organizational management will increase, posing problems for leaders. Allow business units to tailor performance management since what works for one section of the company may not work for another. Providing reskilling and career development support—for example, by establishing resources and building up platforms to enable insight into internal jobs—when organizational complexity affects career pathing. The present economic crisis has also stretched the boundaries of how corporations perceive employee satisfaction. Employing such methods can be an effective strategy to improve employees' physical health and emotional well-being. Focus less on jobs — which group unrelated talents — and more on the skills needed to drive the organization's competitive advantage and the processes that fuel that advantage to develop the workforce you'll need post-pandemic. Instead of preparing for a certain future post, encourage individuals to build crucial abilities that might offer various options for their professional advancement. Employees in crucial jobs who lack critical abilities should receive more career development help.

Summing Up

The coronavirus illness of 2019-20 has caught the globe off guard and has had a significant impact on many people's lives, especially those in the business sector and its stakeholders. The post-COVID period is characterized by turmoil and volatility in the commercial world. HR will now play a major role in helping enterprises simplify their operations, create their strategy, and hire more effectively. Organizations must improve flexibility and adapt to the changing needs of the business world as a result of technological advancements and organizational reorganization. Leaders must be willing to adjust goals and designs when company objectives shift. Agile product ownership and backlog management strategies might aid in this situation. While the COVID epidemic emphasizes the importance of agility and speed in the workplace, it's critical to remember that it's not about completing everything at breakneck speed. Leaders who could adjust to unpredictability were differentiated from those who couldn't. As the epidemic fades, mergers and acquisitions (M & A) and company nationalization will accelerate.

CHAPTER THREE

MINDSET & FORWARD-THINKING

Thinking Ahead To Invest In The Future To Implement Lasting Organizational Solutions

"I can't change the direction of the wind, but I can adjust my sails to always reach my destination."-Jimmy Dean

Adaptive capacity refers to a person's ability to cope with change and challenges to the status quo. It also includes how a person responds to situational circumstances with suitable actions rather than default inclinations and behaviors. When company executives recognize that the circumstances are in charge, they may choose actions that boost their adaptability. As a result, leadership becomes more adaptable. Because the future is fundamentally unpredictable, adaptable leadership is essential for long-term success. COVID-Leaders who could adjust to unpredictability were differentiated from those who couldn't. Conventional companies, the person in charge of making operational choices, particularly major ones, is the person at the top. The leader of flexible organizations works on creating the suitable atmosphere. In the case of the airport, the board's ability to focus on finding the best pilots and co-pilots while resisting the urge to co-design solutions was absolutely extraordinary. They trusted their staff, gradually let go of the reins in a measured manner, and were rewarded with powerful, inventive ideas that came from within the company.

The coronavirus illness of 2019 (COVID-19) has caught the globe off guard and has had a significant impact on many people's lives, especially those in the business sector and its stakeholders. Many businesses have been pushed to their limits, and in some cases, to the brink of bankruptcy, in the previous year. Their systems have disintegrated due to intense strain on operations, supply chains, and demand, and any notion of collaboration among their ranks has been tossed to the wind. Working in crisis mode is, of course, neither sustainable nor desirable. Many company executives are now wondering how they can maintain momentum post-crisis and ensure their firms' future adaptability. How can people transition from crisis mode to proactive thinking? The secret is to maintain a constant state of flexibility. Every business leader understands that in order to thrive in the long run, their organization must adapt. The true challenge isn't effectively converting your firm on a one-time basis; it's writing the capacity to adapt and transform into the DNA of the company. It's about creating a mechanism or reaction to cope with any crisis that arises, whether it's a financial, technical, environmental, or health-related one.

But how do businesses become high-performance businesses? You all know that organizational and people skills drive financial and operational success and enable firms to execute their plans, yet the majority of businesses have no idea how to quantify them. Future leaders with talents that are suited to future requirements are in the pipeline. Leaders in high-performance businesses have been nurtured for success by rotating through various sorts of jobs and responsibilities in various functions and areas. These organizations discover and develop prospective leaders early in their careers. According to a survey of more than 5,000 executives conducted by The Boston Consulting Group and the World Federation of People Management Associations, high-performing organizations fill 60% of top-management positions with internal candidates, while low-performing organizations fill only 13%.

"Each sad family is miserable in its own unique manner, while all happy families—or high-performing organizations—are the same."-Tolstoy

All businesses may place themselves in a better position to succeed by knowing the common strands of organizational DNA. These real-world circumstances have a role in organizational transformation, allowing flexible businesses to make progress while others struggle to establish ground rules and goals. Adaptable businesses value themselves and the environment in which they operate. They don't strive to separate themselves from this environment; instead, they thrive in it. Survivors are highly adaptive groups. They were the ones that embraced change before it wrecked them, riding the wave while others battled against it. Adaptable organizations are those that not only survive a change in the hope of flowing back into serenity in the current economic conditions, which are crippled by numerous lockdowns and heaving under changing restrictions every few weeks. Organizational flexibility, on the other hand, allows them to accept more of these changes and make them work by altering their working model to meet the new requirements.

The difficulty is that, despite the effort put out by business executives, most attempts to make organizations adaptive fail. The author's personal experience working in management and as a strategy consultant supports this. When you ask senior executives what went wrong, you'll hear the same concerns again and over: Some employees inside the company neglected to accept responsibility for the transition process. People began blaming one another. Nothing was done about it when things went wrong. The metamorphosis slowed down over time.For many flexible firms, profit plans have been replaced by promises of company continuity. Many businesses put long-term aspirations on hold to meet the needs of a workforce concerned about their future, stakeholders facing unpredictable demands, and operational obstacles. The challenge of labor planning is mitigated to some extent in industries where remote employment is available. However, it will necessitate more unlearning and upskilling. While some businesses balked at the new expectations owing to a lack of digital preparedness, purpose-driven businesses maintained spirits high and order volumes high by delivering online.

The encouraging reality is that people who have been dealing with fear and uncertainty for more than a year demonstrate an unbreakable spirit. Adaptive organizations' teams didn't rely on adrenaline; instead, they pushed themselves forward, appreciative of the positions they had and what they could do online if they couldn't meet their coworkers in person. To make teleworking feasible, business agility was followed to the letter and in spirit; a variety of virtual collaboration technologies were extensively utilized; and figures were tracked with the same earnestness as before the epidemic. Several of the flexible working concepts and policy modifications implemented during the pivotal period of uncertainty and emergency firefighting are still in place. Why? simply because they provide outcomes and keep flexible businesses on track with progress.

The issue is that tighter restrictions may suffocate an organization. In truth, management should relinquish control and allow the business the flexibility it requires to function efficiently. The concept is that management should focus on stating their goals and letting the company figure out how to get there. It might be difficult to let go of your grasp while not allowing the firm to fall apart. It must be founded on a defined set of concepts that are supported by science.

Treating an adaptive task as a technical challenge is one of the most common leadership blunders. Leadership requires knowing when to solve problems and when to learn. *"We often look for technical answers to problems,"* author explains. But there's also all the adjusting that has to be done. It does not tackle the problem at its root without adaptive work. Identifying the fundamental difficulties in an adaptive challenge focuses on areas where individuals may differ, and this disagreement becomes a roadblock to development. In this instance, leaders must evaluate the following factors: Competing values or priorities. There are legacy issues that must be addressed. Issues or procedures that remain ambiguous or perplexing over time

The author observes that individuals do not fight change. Instead, they fight against loss, which may take various forms, including material loss, as well as loss of competence and loyalty. When people are dealing with significant losses, they are frequently resistant to change, author explains. According to him , in adaptive settings, leaders may begin to comprehend the problem by first understanding the people. Leaders are aware of the sacrifices they are asking people to make. Even if it's only noting and naming those parts and losses, it's vital to honor them. Start visualizing people's anxieties and what's at stake. Someone is afraid of losing something because you perceive the improvements you are attempting to make as generally beneficial on the surface. Keep an open mind and seek out new perspectives. It is necessary to first learn about the perspectives of those who will be affected by the change in order to create an adaptive change. Consider the following questions: What are their core values?

The author advises that just asking smart questions and following guided procedures does not imply that the change is not being implemented. Instead, acknowledging and commemorating the losses is part of the leadership plan, followed by moving forward with a deeper meaning of them. Making headway on difficult problems" COVID-19, societal difficulties, and conflicts have all necessitated making quick modifications in the previous two years. Moving forward with these complex issues puts new strains on your abilities and encourages us to develop at the cutting edge of your abilities. You'll need new tools, frameworks, and solutions to do so. explains Accepting responsibility for assisting others in achieving a common goal in the face of adversity is key. The ability to remain calm in the face of adversity is crucial. That is why, in today's world, you require this style of leadership. Over the years, leadership has evolved from a technical process to a much more adaptable one, requiring figuring out how to assist people deal with uncertainty.

According to the author, the inclusion of *"uncertainty"* in the concept of leadership is a plus since it means that one does not have to know all of the answers. In reality, you can't fix it yourself as a leader in an adaptive environment. All you can do is assist your group in making growth, and that is a success. Taking on a variety of challenges you survive by solving challenges that emerge in the lives of your groups, whether it's an organization, a community, a patient, or an institution. However, you must consider the nature of the task you are confronted with. The problem is well-known, easy to recognize, and frequently identifiable based on prior experience. The solution is well-known based on prior experience and knowledge. Obstacles are frequently restricted in terms of resources, such as time and money.

The problem is frequently unknown or difficult to define; it is linked to underlying patterns or dynamics and necessitates learning. The remedy is also unknown, necessitating learning. Those who are affected by the challenge (stakeholders), including authorities, have responsibility. The barriers are more intangible: hearts and minds, ideals, loyalty, and connections. Adaptive difficulties are the most difficult because of the leadership techniques. According to the author, adaptive change necessitates leaders successfully narrating and anchoring individuals on what will remain constant and what will need to change. There are a few more things you may do to help. By taking a step back, leaders may observe all of the numerous variables that surround a problem. Observe, pause for thought, interpret, and then intervene in the process's next stage. Identify what has been lost, give people time to process it, and then help them move on with their lives. Everyone involved in the shift is tense or disturbed in some way at any given time, according to the author. Learning threshold beyond which no one learns anything or makes a difference. There is also a point at which people's tolerance for change reaches a breaking point. The zone of productive disequilibrium, is the ideal range of suffering within which the urgency of the system pushes people to participate in adaptive labor. You make issues about individuals so often but people are merely showing various viewpoints on a challenge. Leaders must comprehend the opinions of others rather than taking it personally, and they must develop bridges across divides—especially with those who disagree with you or who would try to stifle or reject progress. You're all going through waves of uncertainty right now, and your role as leaders isn't to fix it for people; it's to help them cope with it, move through it, and discover something deeper. It is critical to implement both technical and adaptive changes. Just make sure you don't mix them up—do both.

Leadership Challenges

Hesitancy Change can only be successful if everyone in the organization is involved in its execution. Some employees may be unwilling to execute a new approach because it requires them to master a new method or alters the nature of their work. It is possible that a new strategy will be unsuccessful if it is not applied across the whole organization. Power Adaptive leadership transfers authority and influence from a few top-level executives to all employees. Some top-level workers who are accustomed to wielding a great deal of decision-making authority may find it difficult to give control to the entire group.

While maintaining a positive environment, adaptive leadership may provide businesses with inventive and meaningful answers to challenging situations. Adaptive leadership, on the other hand, can provide a number of obstacles, including: Adaptive leadership necessitates the participation of all members of the organization. This implies adaptable leaders must urge everyone engaged to change their mentality and display adaptive leadership skills. Employees who prefer the status quo and have no desire to change the company may find this difficult. Adaptive leadership's proactive character necessitates the recognition that some of the organization's existing business processes are unproductive. Adaptive leadership, poses a number of difficulties. Experimenting, learning new information, and making multiple modifications throughout your firm are all part of this leadership paradigm. You will only be able to maintain the changes and prosper if you modify your mindset and adjust your policies.

Changing people's attitudes, beliefs, and perceptions, on the other hand, is frequently more difficult than flossing a cat's teeth. Making adjustments necessitates a degree of disloyalty to your past. If you wish to adopt a new marketing plan, for example, you must first accept the truth that your current marketing techniques are ineffective. Another issue with adaptive leadership is that it creates an environment conducive to various types of opposition. This might be from your employees or other stakeholders in the organization. Stakeholder Any individual, group, or entity with an interest in an organization and the effects of its activities is referred to as a stakeholder in business. typical clientele or circumstancesMarginalizing, distracting, and assaulting are the most prevalent techniques used to stymie adaptive change. If you see any of these behaviors, it's likely that your staff are resisting the new policy you're attempting to impose. The refusal of leaders to listen to other people's perspectives is perhaps the biggest obstacle posed by adaptive leadership. Adaptive leadership, as previously said, is more about cooperation than it is about power.

Adaptive workplaces may become even more appealing in a post-pandemic environment. Employees have a say in where they work, shaping the dialogue, shaping the workplace, and eventually impacting leadership choices, which is a key part of adaptable workplaces. Employees' well-being, passion for the job, and dedication to the firm are all enhanced when they have a sense of choice and control over when, how, and where they conduct their work. Here are a few instances of workplaces that are adaptable: Siemens has stated that its workers would be able to work two or three days a week from wherever they feel most productive. Employees at Twitter may work from anywhere in the world at any time. With no top-down-driven minimum need for in-office work, most professionals and project teams at Deloitte establish the adaptable working environment that works best for them and their clients. Improved work/life balance and reduced stress: reports of reduced stress and burnout, as well as increased productivity and more time to focus on family support, as a result of the ability to telework or work remotely, even for one or two days per week. The author feels that working online allows her to be much more attentive to clients, and that saving time on travelling allows her to engage more clients while feeling motivated. Virtual touchpoints approach to virtual communication with families, such as short phone calls or text updates, to help her establish connections in preparation for longer visits and more intensive chats that improved interaction with teenagers and young people. According to anecdotal evidence, virtual communication channels are especially effective with teenagers and young people.

To make work easier for everyone, your team agreed on which tasks should be done collectively and which should be done separately. The team, for example, decided that planning activities should be done jointly but that targeted activities, such as data analysis, should be done alone. They might organize collaborative activities on their team's co-located days by doing this for a variety of projects. Making virtual watercoolers a possibility: While there is no alternative to face-to-face conversations, there are techniques to replicate comparable, spontaneous encounters in a virtual environment. You and your colleagues use a range of channels to enable seamless collaboration between co-located and remote workers.

One of adaptive leadership's strengths is also one of its limitations. For the most part, an adaptable leader must place less value on structure in order to efficiently execute change. Some employees, on the other hand, thrive in regimented workplaces, and adaptive leadership would be a poor match for them. An adaptable leader will attempt to provide some structure for those employees that require it. Nonetheless, in this unstructured work environment, there are still possibilities for individuals to be less productive.It's in the nature of rules to be broken. An ethical leader may squirm after seeing how an adaptable leader operates. Ethical leaders support an organization's policies because they correspond with their own personal beliefs. An adaptable leader, on the other hand, may bend (or even break) the laws within the bounds of the law in order for the business to undertake the most effective change plan feasible.

The definition of leadership is someone who enjoys making decisions and is concerned about whether their judgments will result in desirable results in the face of uncertainty. Whether a leader is equipped for core, effective, or adaptive leadership depends on how comfortable and enjoyable it is for them to make difficult unilateral decisions. How many times have you heard a leader remark, *"That's policy,"* without telling you where it says so or letting you know what you can anticipate from the policy? A staffer, from the author's perspective, is a leader who perceives a problem and responds with typical replies rather than attempting to find a solution. Accept failure. Adaptive leaders aren't afraid of failure. Adaptive leaders create environments that encourage experimentation, learning, and reflection on both success and failure. Adaptive leaders aren't afraid of failure. Adaptive leaders and their teams become more resilient as a result of their adaptability. They get stronger as a result of their blunders. Leaders who keep going and endure in the face of adversity attain success. When they stop trying, they call it *"failure."* Failure is viewed as a learning opportunity by adaptive leaders, and experimentation is praised even if the desired objective is not reached. The important thing is to keep going ahead. It's critical to figure out why something failed quickly and then move on.

If they aren't making errors, the adaptive leader believes they aren't working hard enough. Successful corporations that accept failure are Netflix, Amazon, and Coca-Cola. You can't learn unless you fail, and you can't achieve until you face obstacles. Adaptive leaders allow everyone to make mistakes. It will re-energize a company.

> *"I have not failed," Thomas Edison is reported as saying. I've come up with 10,000 methods that won't work. "*

You are enthusiastic about empowering individuals and

organizations to thrive in the face of continual and disruptive change, and you accomplish this via programs that address organizational change, resilience, agility, leadership, transformation, and adaptation. Strong organizations are what make the difference for successful businesses. How can you create a healthy workplace? Make sure you have a coherent leadership team, that the leadership team has a common purpose, that you overcommunicate that objective to all employees, and that you reinforce it in all human processes. Traditional leadership training methods appear to take individuals as they are and turn them into leaders by talking to them about leadership concepts and abilities. There is some self-exploration, but the author's impression is that the courses move on to the notion of leadership relatively rapidly, with less emphasis on self-exploration as a leader. That's not a problem. However, in the author's opinion, who you are is the most important component in defining the type of leader you will be. Your training as integrated coaches supports this viewpoint. You strive to figure out who you are and what it entails for your leadership style and decisions. When you engage with your executive customers to help them develop their businesses, When you work with your executive clients to help them become more adaptable leaders, you start by figuring out who they are—what their personality type is, how they handle stress, how they communicate, what they value, and so on. All of this is in the service of gaining a better understanding of themselves as individuals and then implementing the notion of leadership in light of that knowledge.

Leadership is in short supply in both developed and emerging sectors, where aging executives are leaving and new markets are struggling to keep up with fast development. Because of today's rapid speed of change, command and control leadership has become obsolete. Effective leaders think strategically, set the tone, manage resources, foster involvement, hold people accountable, and produce outcomes. In good times, let alone in uncertain ones, there are no simple techniques. Leadership begins at the top of the pyramid but does not end there. Three major levers are used by high-performance businesses to develop leaders at all levels. Leaders in high-performance teams generate urgency and direction. Complexity, volatility, and change are all familiar to leaders. They can mobilize the organization in the face of uncertainty. Although imaginative leaders are required, they cannot be lone wolves or independent operators; the heroic corporate leader's days are past. Today's leaders must collaborate with their colleagues and appreciate the collective power that comes from teamwork. They must increasingly be at ease working with outsiders such as nonprofit groups, regulators, and other bodies that are more involved in business.

Although research into the influence of COVID-19 on organizational structure, job design, and employee well-being has increased, few studies have looked into the importance of leadership and what it takes to be a successful leader under such circumstances. Using the COVID-19 crisis as a case study, this study combines social cognition theory and conservation of resources theory to argue for the role of adaptable personalities in the creation of competent leaders during times of crisis. You contend that managers with an adaptable personality have higher levels of self-efficacy for leading during a crisis, resulting in higher motivation to lead during the COVID-19 crisis.

Furthermore, it is suggested that managers with increased motivation to lead during the COVID-19 crisis have improved adaptive performance, implying a serial mediation model in which crisis leader self-efficacy and motivation to lead during the COVID-19 crisis act as explanatory mechanisms of the relationship between the adaptive personality and the manager's performance. To test author's hypothesis, he gathered data from more than 100 full-time managers in India during the COVID-19 crisis and analyzed it using hierarchical linear regression. All of the hypotheses are supported by the findings. It includes a discussion of the findings, contributions, limits, and future directions. Covid-19 has had a significant impact on the globe in a variety of fields and businesses.

Changes in the implementation of a country's education system are one of COVID-19's significant impacts. The school authorities had to cope with a variety of concerns and obstacles that arose as a result of the debate. Changes in the media and teaching techniques employed at the school level, as well as in other educational institutions, demonstrate this. To maintain the continuity of teaching and learning, school administrators should adopt a proactive approach. As a result, this study discusses adaptive leadership, resilience development, and leadership duty distribution. In addition, this report discusses some novel culture-fostering methods for school leaders to use during the COVID-19 endemic phase. The findings suggest that school leaders should take action and influence the school atmosphere so that the school ecosystem can work together to address the situation. Adaptive Leadership and Continuous Improvement The concept of *"continuous improvement"* appears straightforward, but it needs a skilled leader to make it work.

Thinking Forward

Trust is more fundamental than any other aspect of an organization's code of ethics. Employees that are trustworthy appreciate the challenge and honor of being a valued part of an organization's day-to-day struggles and accomplishments. They repay the confidence placed in them by demonstrating their commitment to the organization when it is most in need. When everything is up in the air, individuals are stronger when they stick together and help one another in modest steps toward a common goal. These modifications should be led by designated changemakers. Honest debates and even spontaneous exchanges of ideas can aid in the advancement of change. Experiment, test, and record change: It's no secret that in times of significant change, flexible businesses rely on essential individuals they can trust. It takes more than a strong willingness to ride through change to turn it into a consistent, practical model with a roadmap and quantifiable goals. Clients and stakeholders are frequently concerned that sensitive information may fall into the wrong hands when teams access databases remotely. For major enterprises or even small businesses to contemplate workforce flexibility, additional levels of security in the form of masking, network support, and encryption are essential. Crash courses and hands-on learning, which are typically done alone, provide the vital aspect of adaptation to this massive shift in working and engagement styles. The youthful workforce in India is fearless of change. According to a study, 53% of workers would consider changing occupations if it meant more flexibility on the job. You can sense the difference when you come into a high-performing organization. People are energised rather than going through the motions. Rather than being puzzled or resigned, they are confident in their organization's direction and the changes that are taking place. They understand what they are meant to be doing and how it connects to their neighbors' activities. Checking performance measurements like sustained profitability and market share growth at firms, as well as social impact in the charity arena, can swiftly validate your informal findings.

Organizational design may assist businesses in improving execution and achieving strategic objectives. However, the interaction of its essential elements—structure, personal talents, responsibilities, and collaboration—must be properly organized and intimately integrated with a company's strategy and sources of competitive advantage for this to happen. A well-designed structure should stress the most important aspects of a company. It is difficult to accommodate all dimensions evenly in the real world. For example, a corporation concentrating on future success in major markets can arrange its operations by area rather than channel. Even while channels did not represent the main axis in the firm, its leaders would need to make cautious efforts to guarantee that they were receiving sufficient support. The structure of an organization should also be dynamic, focusing on current and future objectives rather than legacy priorities. An organization's structure may need to be adjusted as strategy, performance, or the competitive environment change. Organizations with lean architecture may focus on meaningful work rather than coordinating. Activities that do not provide value are removed. Communication and decision-making are faster with fewer organizational levels, and senior executives have a clearer picture of day-to-day operations and consumer interactions. Managers become more ambitious in using their leadership talents as their spans of influence become larger. They don't have time to micromanage, but they may gain confidence in their leadership, coaching, and inspiring abilities. Although lean firms have a reduced cost base, the additional benefits of success outweigh the financial ones.

The capacity to evolve in two key ways creates a persistent competitive advantage in today's fast-paced environment. To begin, businesses must take a methodical approach to driving changes in focus, strategy, direction, structure, and culture. Second, they must have the ability to quickly respond to changing market conditions. Change is a methodical process. Despite the high failure rate of change initiatives, a few firms are succeeding. They make certain that the leadership team is on the same page about the firm's goals and strategies for change, and they intentionally convey that alignment to employees layer by layer throughout the organization.

Summing Up

Adaptable businesses value themselves and the environment in which they operate. They don't strive to separate themselves from this environment; instead, they thrive in it. Adaptive change requires leaders to observe, pause for thought, interpret, and intervene in the process's next stage. Obstacles are restricted in terms of resources, such as time and money; barriers are more intangible: hearts and minds, ideals, loyalty, and connections. Adaptive difficulties are the most difficult because of the leadership techniques. Adaptive leadership may provide businesses with inventive and meaningful answers to challenging situations. The author's view is that who you are is the most important component in defining the type of leader you will be. Effective leaders think strategically, set the tone, manage resources, foster involvement, and produce outcomes. In times of significant change, flexible businesses rely on essential individuals they can trust. A corporation concentrating on future success in major markets can arrange its operations by area rather than channel. Managers become more ambitious in using their leadership talents as their spans of influence become larger. Lean firms have a reduced cost base, but the additional benefits of success outweigh the financial ones. Despite the high failure rate of change initiatives, a few firms are succeeding.

CHAPTER FOUR

STRATEGIC THINKING

A Systematic Approach To Determining The Need For Changes

"If you're walking down the right path, and you're willing to keep walking, eventually you will make progress." - Barack Obama

Today, no sector or company is immune to disruption, yet many companies are ill-equipped to adapt rapidly enough to withstand the consequences of rapid change. In the second year of the pandemic, the workplace became a fraught battleground, with employees seeing opportunities to rethink what they wanted out of work and participating in the so-called great resignation and employers attempting to define a new normal while COVID-19 and its variants wreaked havoc on even the best-laid plans. You looked for companies that were either providing the kinds of tools that were designed to create a thriving, positive environment regardless of whether work was done in person, hybrid, or fully remote, or that inherently understood the nature of this tumult and adapted their policies and approaches to serve employees in this charged environment. You are continuously on the lookout for new trends to keep up with.

The COVID-19 epidemic has prompted you to utilize a variety of descriptive terms and phrases, including *"the new normal," "business agility," "adaptability," and "flexibility."* These are all over the press and in corporate meetings. Here's why the author believes adaptable best captures the future of a successful company. Adaptive is a fresh take on an old concept. He characterized it as the ability to drastically rethink basic business model, including its core goal, key value proposition, core competences, markets or sectors in which it competes, its ultimate customer. Organizations that understand their surroundings and are positioned to detect and respond to change have the best chance of surviving disruptions. Keeping an eye on your rival is unavoidable. You must actively research how well they are responding to change, as well as how far behind or ahead of them you are. Business leaders must prioritize and encourage flexibility as a must-have organizational quality if they want to position themselves for long-term success in an ever-changing market. Traditional metrics of corporate health are no longer sufficient. To become adaptive now and survive tomorrow, the focus must be on shifting viewpoints and morphing swiftly and at scale. Adopting new business sustainability ideas is one way for organizations to start their journey toward becoming more adaptive and, thus, better prepared for an uncertain future.

Adaptive businesses prioritize a common vision at all levels of the organization, with a strong emphasis on delivering value to customers and the broader stakeholder community. These companies have cultures that are engaged, motivated, and high-performing, and they adjust to change quickly and easily. To drive the evolution of its business, an adaptive organization will constantly analyze and anticipate changes in its market. With an adaptable attitude, these companies respect situational awareness and engage in the design and implementation of digital and data projects to support it. These businesses also utilize data to develop, test, and enhance new value-creating initiatives and business models.

Adaptable organizations minimize superfluous hierarchy by devolving governance and decision-making authority to lower levels. When an organization uses self-organizing, cross-functional teams and has a flexible organizational structure that allows employees to easily move between positions and into quickly morphing team structures, performance, innovation, and responsiveness to change all improve. Sharing authority, prioritizing employee needs, and assisting individuals in developing and performing at their best are all important aspects. Adaptive organizational cultures thrive when leaders provide context, eliminate obstacles, and include team members in strategic choices that affect them. A successful adaptive organization strives to foster justice, constructive conflict, and psychological safety, which fosters trust, shared accountability, variety of opinion, and risk tolerance. These companies' employees are free to express their honest opinions about the business climate and how they feel it will affect the company. An adaptable organization's capacity to grab opportunities as they come – and often even before they arise – is a critical trait. Adoption of technology to modernize and enhance processes, as well as new methods of thinking and working, is required to succeed in these traits. In order to get the competitive advantage that comes with being adaptable, a company is more likely to go through a series of digital evolutions rather than a single transformation. While an evolution signals a step forward in digital modernisation for certain businesses, protracted and costly transformations may not always provide the expected results.

While some firms may be trying to reinvent themselves, the dangers of transition for businesses with huge and complicated structures are extremely significant. The caterpillar-and-butterfly principle that underpins the promise of sweeping digital transformation does not apply to adaptable organizations. Indeed, in a constantly evolving adaptive mindset, digital change can only be achieved in an evolutionary manner as responses to changing market forces, anticipated or new business opportunities, and emerging risks and threats; and can only be addressed if there is digital agility to pivot when and for what is required. To guide their strategy, these companies must be able to continually monitor market signals, customers, rivals, the value chain, and people.

Digitized situational awareness is assisting organizations in being more adaptable. Situational awareness is not just being aware of current events impacting an organization but also being able to contextualize those events in the framework of what is expected in order to understand what they mean, as well as being aware of what is likely to occur in the near future. Situational awareness, in a digital sense, refers to a system of insight that uses all available data pertaining to certain occurrences that must be comprehended holistically and acted upon to achieve the desired change. Situational awareness is not a new idea, but its use in modern business is rapidly growing. Organizations that want to be more nimble might benefit from digitized situational awareness. An agile team's alignment to the customer value stream, as well as its proximity to customer interactions, guarantees that it can continuously sense consumer behavior and give insights to guide the next iteration of a company's market proposal, for example.

Organizations are beginning to leverage their growing volumes of data to produce insights that will help them make better decisions. However, because of the magnitude and complexity of the data, reliable, actionable, and timely information that might provide a competitive edge is difficult to gather. An adaptable company that is always monitoring and anticipating changes in its competitive environment requires reliable and accurate information. Leading companies collect and translate data into easily digestible operational, customer, market, and risk signals on a regular basis. These signals are the analytic building blocks that AI systems employ to increase prediction accuracy in the context of expected outcomes in order to improve situational awareness. In order to accomplish the requisite dynamic agility, the supporting technology must also be digitally agile. IT systems must not only be available everywhere and simple to use, but they must also be easily modified, developed, or replaced to meet new market problems. Situational awareness, real-time signals and insights, and contemporary and adaptable technology all complement and increase the impact of each capacity. An organization that takes this comprehensive strategy will achieve more than it could with just one or two of these talents.

No questions are avoided in highly adaptable companies, and no subjects are deemed too sensitive to discuss. There is a shared responsibility for the organization's future. In many ways, adaptive organizations demonstrate a sense of shared responsibility for the whole: they frequently engage in cross-functional problem-solving, people feel free to discuss issues outside their purview at meetings, and the compensation and reward system reflects shared accountability for the company's performance. The ability to make independent decisions is appreciated and anticipated. Managers at the highest levels talk about topics that aren't related to their functional responsibilities. After participating in robust give and take, people may modify their beliefs and attitudes in a free and open debate.

Courageous leaders with a long-term view and a commitment to the organization's future lead adaptive organizations. They have solid talent pipelines and succession strategies in place. Leaders are generally created by participation in and reflection on real-world situations, which are supported by additional training and development activities. Reflection and lifelong learning are ingrained in the culture. Most of today's intractable problems are beyond the knowledge and competence of even the most seasoned professionals. Learning is one of the most important qualities in today's environment, and an adaptable organization is receptive to it. Front-line perspectives are considered in strategic decision-making; mistakes are not punished; retreats and opportunities to reflect are routine and include a cross-section of the organization; breakdowns are treated as opportunities to learn; collaboration across all boundaries is encouraged; strategic plans are respected but not treated as sacred and unchangeable texts.

Adaptive organization necessitates initiatives that engage individuals in your system to address important issues. These interventions have a few characteristics: they forgo fast fixes in favor of long-term solutions; they make people uncomfortable, but they use the discomfort to build traction; they establish and employ new networks of connections; and they improve the organization's overall adaptive ability. Slowing down the organization from moving too quickly and reflecting before acting is often the most useful thing you can do. Ask more questions, withhold your support for a decision until the right time, add extra time to meeting agendas to discuss the adaptive challenge, expand the circle of stakeholders, and separate distracting arguments from the real issues underlying the adaptive issue are some of the useful ways to do this.

Adaptability to changing circumstances is a must-have attribute for today's businesses, especially in this unpredictable environment. Adaptability is a must-have organizational attribute for business executives. There is no assurance that the biggest and fiercest industry incumbents will survive as disruption intensifies. Adaptiveness is built on innovation, and encouraging individuals to think outside the box is critical to achieving it. In every case, these companies have shown an exceptional capacity to adjust swiftly to shifting circumstances. These businesses are well positioned to succeed in unpredictable times, both now and in the future, with the correct strategy and grit. Many factors will influence an organization's future health, including changes based on area, industry, and even company type. To keep fit while acquiring dynamic competitive advantages, the unifying thread is to focus on revolutionary business drivers. Consider the human dimension while building business models, products, and services for all company stakeholders. Encourage innovation by researching new ideas ahead of time and supporting innovative corporate cultures. Develop a solid digital transformation plan to keep up with technological improvements and to stay ahead of any possible disruption. Any flexible and future-ready company will have these characteristics. This preparation will allow companies to respond more swiftly to changes in client needs, technological developments, and disturbing competition than companies that rely solely on size and efficiency. Many other internal and external factors may limit a company's capacity to adapt, but greater planning and transformation may serve as a roadmap for executives wishing to avoid the same blunders that have brought other businesses to their knees.

Businesses should consider the future as a continuum rather than a binary decision between onsite and virtual. Instead, they should seek to establish flexible, adaptable workplaces where people and teams may move about as required, depending on the nature of the job and where they and their teams are most effective. When scenarios involving dependents and childcare become more normalized and social isolation is reduced, adaptive workplaces may become even more appealing in a post-pandemic environment. The first step is to distinguish between the dissatisfied now that your organization was created to solve and the ideal future that it strives to achieve. This aim requires clarity and consensus. It has to be a common mental model. Second, this future aim or state must be intrinsically motivating, serving as a source of inspiration and ambition for everyone in the company throughout both normal and difficult times. Third, visions work best when they are brief and straightforward. A complicated paragraph is unlikely to inspire, and it is more likely to include empty words or jargon exclusive to one's industry that everyone is sick of hearing. Fourth, the vision should be quantifiable. This planned future state must be specific enough that a statistic or metrics can tell you when and if you've arrived. Microsoft's initial ambition was to have " *a computer on every desk and in every household.*" The most significant mental model of every organization is its vision, which is the intended objective or future state that the company wants.

The list of brick-and-mortar companies having to compete against more nimble online competitors continues to expand, from Toys R Us to Austin Reed to HMV. What about the enterprises that were able to adapt? Here are top picks for companies that have stayed relevant, predicted trends, and embraced innovation. Do you recall the days when you could rent DVDs? Netflix was founded in 1997 by CEO Reed Hastings and began by shipping

DVDs to consumers. It's difficult to fathom without viewing video on demand now that there are over 109 million customers globally. Hastings had the idea in 2001 to transmit movies directly to our televisions over the internet. He experimented for several years to get clients used to streaming rather than watching actual DVDs. Hastings has always dreamed big, but he started small, failed swiftly, and grew rapidly. Netflix has perfected the disruptive innovator's art, producing and authoring its own original blockbuster blockbusters in addition to those created by others. Netflix, which now ranks alongside Facebook, Amazon, and Google as one of the world's leading tech innovators, has revolutionized the way you consume entertainment. Has it broken ties with traditional television networks? What about the big screen's chances of surviving?

You realized that continuous improvement is not the linear process that many people think it is; rather, it requires a great deal more leadership talent, connection-building, political acumen, judgment, and personal touch. The author discovered that both business and health care have understood that continuous improvement strategies do not implement themselves as you read the literature in these fields. Culture-building and leadership of the proper sort are required. At the same time, the author discovered that using continuous improvement methodologies in business or organizational learning poses some unique problems. It can be especially difficult for business schools to generate the type of continuing, collaborative, and learning-oriented work that continuous improvement involves, given the absence of widely acknowledged goals and benchmarks in learning or education, strong traditions of privacy in the classroom, unstable politics, and more. Despite these obstacles, the author found examples of organization that have used continuous improvement-based techniques to promote learning. As it turned out, they were all anchored by an adaptable leader, one who pushed for change while remaining flexible and adept at navigating the context. Such leaders understand how to create long-term initiatives that operate with rather than against the school's persistent rhythms.

Emily Weiss, a former Vogue fashion editor, founded the Into the Gloss beauty blog in 2010, which revolutionized the way women communicate about beauty. For years, Weiss would sit on the bathroom floors of famous people and question them about their beauty rituals, even if they claimed they didn't have one. Weiss leveraged her meticulously chosen editorial platform, as well as the innumerable conversations it spurred, to establish Glossier, the first global beauty company, in 2014. She created a content-driven brand that was fueled by an online community. Weiss used the power of online storytelling to ask her followers what items they wanted Glossier to produce, putting the client at the center of the Glossier universe. The corporation would then produce them based on the comments received. Everything Glossier makes is intended to spark a digital conversation, and certain items had waiting lists of up to 10,000 people last year. Glossier is breaking the norms in the cosmetics industry by turning every client into an influencer, despite the fact that it started small and doesn't sell to retailers.

The way people live, work, and conduct business will continue to be shaped and reshaped by long-term upheaval and change. Adaptive firms must look beyond incremental development and address current practices' flaws on a regular basis. Adaptive leaders need to climb up on the roof from time to time to observe what's coming over the horizon. When they detect the potential for disruption, they must move rapidly to plan responses in concert with other leaders. One such disruption is the proliferation of consumer options and the use of digital technology to differentiate them. It brings with it new opportunities as well as new problems. It's not enough to use digital technology on the periphery.

Organizations must develop new methods of working and productivity metrics. Such new ways of working need a level of leadership competency that has not previously been highlighted or rewarded. When faced with disruption, leaders are put to the test, and they frequently respond in one of two ways: some perceive danger and shut down, while others apply unquestioned know-how rather than taking an adaptive approach by defining or reframing challenges, exploring new domains, and creating.

There are countless examples of once-dominant businesses that failed to sustain their supremacy owing to their failure to adapt to changing circumstances. Consider the case of Kodak. The firm, which was once dominant owing to its photographic films, was sluggish in adapting to digital photography and had to sell many of its patents to stay afloat. Organizations that seek to prevent a similar fate should use the adaptive leadership approach.According to Darwin's Origin of Species, the species that survives is the one that can adapt and adjust to the changing environment in which it finds itself, not the most intelligent or the strongest. While the above remark relates to the significance of adaptability for a species' existence, companies must also be able to adapt to changing conditions.

Technical problems might be difficult to address, but they always present a clear problem that can be handled using current knowledge and the experience of a few experts. For example, if your computer isn't working properly, you may have a professional from your company's IT department fix it for you. Adaptive problems, on the other hand, lack a clearly defined problem and necessitate solutions that are outside of the organization's present competence and know-how.

If an organization is repeatedly confronted with the same type of crisis, for example, it is most likely experiencing adaptation difficulties. Adaptive leadership is based on four key ideas, which we've mentioned here. Organizational fairness Adaptive issues, as previously said, rarely have a clear problem and solution. As a result, fixing them necessitates imagination and inventiveness. As a result, it is critical for an adaptable leader to foster an environment in which all views and opinions are heard. Not only does this result in more innovative ideas, but being a part of the change process also helps individuals feel appreciated. This results in a higher level of buy-in, which is necessary for the solution to be implemented successfully.

Starting with helping leaders understand the business, including its goals, mission, and goods and services, there are six activities and numerous keys to producing adaptable leaders. Form an instructional design team made up of leaders from all levels and create a framework for discussion and creation of leadership training that senior leaders can utilize to ensure that everyone in the company understands what is essential to them and what is required of them. Give key objectives to the instructional design team that oversees human resources, corporate communications, employee relations, and other departments. This should be included in the whole employee experience, from recruiting to retirement.

Empower the instructional design team to lead corporate strategy, program management, operational excellence, and other teams in aligning target setting, investment portfolio management, and other goal-to-results approaches in order to maintain alignment as conditions change. Design, develop, and implement leadership development programs that are iteratively designed, developed, and deployed by the leaders who engaged in steps one through three above. Iterate on material based on the most important aspirations and intents. Leaders must be re-engaged in order to continue their education. Engage learners in refining learning content as the deployment continues by giving application examples, new application scenarios, and hazards. Baseline indicators of employee engagement and sentiment, such as individual experiences with diversity, equity, and inclusion, job value, leadership quality, and teamwork, are used to assess their effects. The capacity to detect and successfully control one's own emotions, as well as the ability to do the same for others, is referred to as emotional intelligence. Adaptive solutions frequently involve individuals letting go of old habits, learning new skills, and adapting to a new way of functioning. This may be an unpleasant procedure, evoking difficult emotions and a sense of loss in a variety of people. Adaptive leadership necessitates the leader's awareness of these intricacies and a mature, intelligent response to them. Expansion Another key aspect of adaptive leadership is learning new things, both at an organizational and individual level. Because adaptive difficulties can't be handled only by applying current knowledge, the people driving the change must be willing to try new techniques, learn from their mistakes, and develop new ways to tackle the problem at hand.

Changing and adjusting is challenging, and it can result in anxiety and other negative emotions. A leader must pace change so that employees are not overwhelmed while maintaining enthusiasm and productivity. Maintain your concentration on the next shift and challenge. Regardless of sideshows, disagreements, or reluctance to change, avoid distractions. Without being sidetracked and losing focus on the adaptive job, the leader must allow for multiple perspectives and initiatives. Gather as much information and viewpoints as possible. At different times and in different ways, people in different parts of an organization will notice changes in the environment and business situations. The leader must avoid becoming an ivory tower by ensuring a flood of knowledge from many sources. People must also be involved in the process of change, be empowered, and share responsibility. Only then will they completely engage and become more adaptable. To some extent, you may do this by adopting a democratic leadership style. Leaders' voices should be protected. Ensure that people are not penalised for expressing their views, even if those views are negative or even dangerous. Punishing individuals for daring to speak their views would diminish creativity and invention because people will be afraid of penalties if they share their ideas and perspectives.

Employee involvement, which has an impact on both efficiency and effectiveness, is overlooked in this mechanical view of production. According to new research, employees who are involved in their job are more productive than those who are not. As the rest of this article suggests, organizations should incorporate this third dimension of productivity—engagement—to lock in the benefits of adaptive workplaces while mitigating the challenges, recognizing that people are typically more efficient and effective when they are more engaged in the work they do . According to Deloitte research, employee engagement is often strongest among workers who work remotely 60–80% of the time. Furthermore, according to a Gallup study, teams with high levels of employee engagement are 21% more productive. These findings are backed up by statistics from the Federal Work Life Survey, which reveals that teleworkers are 16% more engaged, 19% more pleased, and 11% less likely to leave than onsite employees. Telework enhances performance, morale, health, stress management, and the desire to stay with the company, according to the majority of managers and workers. While remote work has its benefits, some professions and activities cannot be completed as quickly or efficiently in a virtual environment. Conducting on-site audits and inspections, dealing with highly sensitive information, maintaining buildings and physical infrastructure, and other tasks requiring the physical movement of items, people, and things are just a few examples. Furthermore, being social creatures, face-to-face human connection and the formation of interpersonal relationships have immense value that is difficult to attain in virtual contexts.

The idea that resilience is crucial to a company's success. Since March, the phrase *"resiliency"* has gotten a lot of attention, and it has a lot to do with uncertainty. A resilient company is designed to adapt to and recover from unexpected occurrences. Investors today value firms based on expected future earnings and some quantifiable risk, but generally ignore Knightian uncertainty. You believe they will in the future. To put it another way, the adaptability (and resiliency) of public firms will directly affect the value of their stock prices. The trend toward investment depending on business outcomes. You're working on a new concept, but the gist is that many companies still use return-on-investment calculations when investing in transformation and technology. Benefits that aren't tangible are greatly undervalued. Adaptive businesses are learning to invest in new ways. They define and invest to accomplish results that match consumer wants or manage risks today or in the near future. This makes it easier for them to adjust when circumstances change. It also enables them to invest in developing robust systems and architectures that allow for future possibilities.

According to a study , one of the most commonly stated success characteristics for managers in was their capacity to evolve and adapt. According to the same study, the inability to evolve and adapt was also one of the most commonly reported causes of failure and derailment among managers in . Before you make a big or little decision, get intrigued, start asking questions, investigate all options, and wonder. This will assist you in identifying a strategy that is superior to the way things have traditionally been done.

Summing UP

Adaptable organizations minimize superfluous hierarchy by devolving governance and decision-making authority to lower levels. A successful adaptive organization strives to foster justice, constructive conflict, and psychological safety. An organization that takes this comprehensive strategy will achieve more than it could with just one or two of these talents. Businesses should consider the future as a continuum rather than a binary decision between onsite and virtual work. The aim of an organization's vision should be to establish flexible workplaces where people and teams may move about as required, depending on the nature of the job and where they and their teams are most effective. Adaptive firms must look beyond incremental development and address current practices' flaws on a regular basis. A leader must pace change so that employees are not overwhelmed while maintaining enthusiasm and productivity. People must also be involved in the process of change, be empowered, and share responsibility. Adaptive businesses are learning to invest in new ways. This makes it easier for them to adjust when circumstances change.

CHAPTER FIVE

NIMBLE CULTURE

To Encourage People's Freedom To Participate In A Collective Vetting Process

"An organization's ability to learn, and translate that learning into action rapidly, is the ultimate competitive advantage."- Jack Welch

Culture helps achieve strategic goals faster. A good organizational culture does not happen by chance. To accomplish strategic goals, high-performance businesses establish, maintain, and monitor a culture. A risk-averse, process-oriented culture with clear lines of authority may be perfectly logical for an airline, but it's a formula for poor performance in an Internet corporation. At each particular time, a company's culture either works or doesn't work for a certain company. Culture should evolve in tandem with strategic aims.

The way things are done in a company reflects the habits and attitudes of its personnel. It is an organization's *"secret sauce,"* bringing a plan to life or killing it. Culture is not set in stone. Cultivating a distinct culture is both achievable and important. Employee engagement, on the other hand, is defined as employees' desire to go above and beyond for a company, not only out of responsibility or for monetary gain, but because work is important to them personally and professionally. Leadership, design, people, and change management are not the same as culture and engagement; culture and engagement are results of the other traits. In the same way that people strengthen their hearts by exercising other bodily muscles, organizations enhance culture and engagement indirectly by working on other traits. Performance management systems, for example, which are part of the people dimension, may have a significant influence on culture.

If COVID-19 has taught business executives anything, it is the difficulty of leading an organization that is not adaptable and flexible in turbulent times. Businesses were forced to deal with unforeseen upheaval and devise solutions on the fly as a result of the epidemic. This adaptability will be critical to success in 2022. This post will explain what adaptive capability is, why it's vital, and how HR can assist leaders in embracing it. It's reasonable to assume that the epidemic threw the corporate world into disarray. Before the epidemic, the rate of change was extraordinary, but the pandemic drove it beyond normalcy. Not only did leaders have to foresee and implement their teams' success, but they also had to be adaptable in order to deal with the wide range of challenges that arose. This ushered in a new age for business, one in which the ability to adapt is crucial to existence. Businesses can no longer rely on traditional long-term strategic direction-setting to compete and expand in an unpredictable, complicated, and ambiguous world. Today's businesses must be able to detect emerging market changes fast and respond swiftly to take advantage of prospective opportunities or resist emerging dangers. Adaptive businesses have the technical and organizational agility to do so, and workplace settings that support resilience, deeper levels of engagement, motivation, cooperation, and autonomy result in improved performance and employee retention.

- Is your company prepared to react to shifting conditions outside your control?
- What can you do as a leader to help your company become more adaptable?

Every time your organization overcomes an adaptable problem, it expands its adaptive capacity and becomes more prepared and equipped to face the next adaptive challenge. You may also improve your organization's adaptability by fostering a flexible culture.

"Starbucks was founded around the experience and the environment of their stores. Starbucks was about a space with comfortable chairs, lots of power outlets, tables and desks at which we could work and the option to spend as much time in their stores as we wanted without any pressure to buy. The coffee was incidental."- Simon Sinek

Senior executives receive feedback from deep inside the business, where the destiny of the change is decided, in order to track progress and make modifications during a large transition. This is known as cascading change. Companies achieve minimal sufficiency by focusing on the most crucial parts of cascading change and doing just enough to succeed without fragmenting focus and effort needlessly. Working in teams that are places of mutual support, where everything is contested without a trace of humiliation, where the critique of individual and team work is encouraged, addressed, and lessons are learned and applied, are all examples of behavior that demonstrates psychological responsibility. Staff who exude confidence in their clients and customers, who *'go the extra mile'* by sharing unsolicited ideas, thoughts, and stimulus, and whose interest in their customers extends beyond respect and service, delivering attentiveness and personal involvement Leaders and supervisors that push their employees, create opportunities for personal growth via new experiences, and treat everyone fairly and with empathy. An organization that is motivated by intellectual, financial, social, and emotional achievement.

Instilling learning culture is another technique to make an organization more adaptive. The rapidity of change, as well as the influence of fast globalization, is a problem for adaptive companies. They attempt to stay one step ahead of their industry's competitors. It is critical to behave effectively and efficiently in addition to working quickly and harder. The only way to behave wisely is to reflect on both accomplishments and mistakes and share lessons learned with all staff. This gives front-line staff the perspective of top executives, which can help them make rapid judgments when they're required the most. In order to achieve company goals, being flexible is preferable to being process-focused. It is critical to promote responsibility in order to achieve adaptation. It's always simpler to blame success on hard work and blame failure on bad luck, but flexible businesses prioritize cultivating and developing a culture of self-accountability. The sense of responsibility guarantees that each member completes obligations with dedication. It fosters a culture of trust and assists the company in avoiding passing on techniques and blame games. Furthermore, the system's viewpoint instills accountability since employees recognize that their actions have consequences.

"Until I came to IBM, I probably would have told you that culture was just one among several important elements in any organization's makeup and success — along with vision, strategy, marketing, financials, and the like... I came to see, in my time at IBM, that culture isn't just one aspect of the game, it is the game.

In the end, an organization is nothing more than the collective capacity of its people to create value."- Louis V. Gerstner,Jr. Former CEO of IBM

A good organizational culture does not happen by chance. To accomplish strategic goals, high-performance businesses establish, maintain, and monitor a culture. A risk-averse, process-oriented culture with clear lines of authority may be perfectly logical for an airline, but it's a formula for poor performance in an Internet corporation. At each particular time, a company's culture either works or doesn't work for a certain company. Culture should evolve in tandem with strategic aims. Personal motivators, like recognition, and performance disciplines, such as performance management measures, are at the core of employee engagement. High-performance firms keep an eye on their employees' pulses, assessing engagement levels on a regular basis and actively managing engagement during challenging periods like restructuring or large-scale change initiatives. Organizations with high performance just operate differently. They recognize the importance of having all traits in their company and work together to put them in place. They also determine which of their trait is the most important for long-term competitive advantage and strive to strengthen weak areas through a systematic set of initiatives and activities.

It all begins with the Board of Directors agreeing that this is the sort of culture they want to see developed. Following agreement, specific procedures must be performed to begin the implementation process. Leaders and managers must collaborate. Leaders and managers must work hard to build a culture of choice, which may be aided by having a description of the current culture in place. An adaptive corporate culture enables a company to respond swiftly and effectively to internal and external change demands. An adaptive corporate culture enables a company to respond swiftly and effectively to internal and external change demands. A business culture that continuously promotes a healthy psychological environment will make employees more stress-resistant. Such a workforce will be able to adjust to change successfully while maintaining productivity. Any organization using the methods detailed in the WellBeing and Performance Agenda must adopt the concepts of adaptive leadership as a top priority, and no change in attitude or practice will occur until someone or several individuals take the initiative. Two elements that underpin the culture of the organization are psychological responsibility and sharing responsibility for the organization's future success.

They have an impact on how individuals interact with one another. Following adaptive leadership, these two agenda items should be implemented. The components of culture that substantially impact trust, commitment, motivation, kinship, focus, and social engagement, the traits that constitute psychologically healthy organizations that function at their peak, are added to adaptive corporate culture. A culture is made up of several components, all of which contribute to the tone, mood, and expectations that surround the workforce and impact their attitude and approach to work. An adaptable corporate culture (adaptive culture) is one that is purposefully developed to generate the tone, mood, and expectations of a psychologically healthy organization, one that encourages employees to feel good. Culture also affects the organization's health.

Jack Welch was correct in his belief that *"learning"* was the driving force behind an adaptable organization. What you now know is that, just as the existence of every creature is dependent on its adaptability to its environment, so is the survival of your organization. So, how exactly do you learn? How can you adapt to your surroundings in order to achieve greater achievements and live longer? The answer is that feedback is how you learn. This leads us to the heart of systems thinking. So let's talk about the systems thinking loop. First, you observe the real world, then you determine which part of the world you want to comprehend, and then you confront whatever problem you are experiencing. It is very important to note that knowing the system in which an issue is embedded is the first step toward resolving it. This allows you to escape the prejudices and biases that hamper your original conceptualization of the situation. It pushes you to spend more time thinking about the framing before you begin solving it. As you are aware, the basis of many difficult situations is your initial framing in the first place. The second thing you must do is create a mental model. That is, express your opinion about the current situation. Third, compare your model to the real world. Examine how your ideas or innovations are faring in the current world, collect data, and keep an eye on things. Fourth, you receive information as feedback. You speak with your workers, clients, and anybody else who is willing to offer their opinions; you record them and use them as data to feed into the new mental model of the scenario. Finally, you restart the loop, interrogating and evolving your mental model. This is the pivotal point in both individual and organizational learning. It also serves as the foundation for design thinking and is crucial to organizational agility, adaptability, survival, and advantage. Every time you walk around the loop, your mental representation of the scenario improves. This means that if your appraisal of the issue is more accurate, any remedy you recommend will be significantly more likely to have an impact. You must be intentional and vocal about the importance of learning in your organization, and you must welcome input from individuals, groups, and the entire organization.This enables your mental models to be constantly updated to reflect reality, making your organization adaptive, agile, and responsive to both internal and external conditions and events of consequence, increasing your likelihood of market dominance and success significantly more than your competition. This means that if your appraisal of the issue is more accurate, any solution you recommend will be significantly more likely to affect the situation and bring about the desired change.

As a leader, you must make a conscious decision to avoid the echo chamber of your own prejudices and views. You must seek out the things you may not want to hear, the harsh criticism and the difficult talk required to handle it. If you accomplish this, your company will become a proponent of adaptability, agility, and continual progress. This will distinguish both your leadership and your firm from the competitors, which is precisely what you want.

Peter Drucker, the father of management, famously said that"culture eats strategy for breakfast."

Culture is strong, but it may feel intangible, like a mystery cloud — that while workers, customers, and partners come and go at different times, an organization's culture endures. The issue is, is culture something that can be consciously built? And the answer is yes, you can construct it and modify it on purpose. When it comes to culture, success is usually due to the sharing of mental models, particularly the most significant mental models such as vision, mission capacity, and learning, among others. And if you don't, you're left with a few well-written sentences and a few maps.

Culture occurs when individuals share the same mental models. This is contrary to the norm of information exchange. You can readily share a PDF or a note, but not your knowledge of things. In other words, you can explain things to people, but you can't make them grasp what you're saying. Given how difficult it is to alter people's hearts and minds, successful leaders gradually create support for the cultural change they desire, rather than trying an organization-wide shift at the outset. Adaptive leaders begin by determining where the work needs to be done and how to appropriately instruct, encourage, and incentivise each employee to create the desired cultural transition.

Those who typically favour the endeavour are referred to as *"supporters,"* while those who are undecided are referred to as "fence-sitters," and those who are opposed are referred to as *"naysayers."* It is also crucial to note that the leaders attempt to incentivize the naysayers, which further perpetuates their conduct. What you propose is to use the success and prizes bestowed on supporters as motivation to proceed along the correct path. Incentives include things like awards, bonuses, and invitations to events. To stimulate action, you then post party photographs to show naysayers everything they're missing. Aside from launching a cultural campaign, CEOs may promote their company's culture in a simple yet powerful way. The key to changing an organization's culture is for CEOs to define and create their own habits to be in alignment with the central tenets of the desired culture.

The CEO of the firm creates and implements a common framework for organizational learning in order to maintain their original startup adaptability as they grow into a larger organization in a rapidly changing environment. And, like many companies, they began as a small team with spontaneous and intimate contact and a rapid synthesis of ideas into action. As the firm expanded to more than 200 people and had a complete management team, conflicting viewpoints on the company's strategic goals began to translate into disparate and unconnected approaches to operational duties. In other words, they were experiencing growing pains. Everyone was working hard, but not all in the same direction.They desired assistance with increasing clarity around their vision and goals; getting everyone in the company on the same page; and identifying and defining organizational capabilities and learning processes. This CEO saw the company's future growth and tried to overcome the conflict between their growing head count and their much-needed scrappy startup traits of speed and adaptability. To do this, the CEO hoped to incorporate adaptability into their business culture. Your astute CEO invited 30 of his top executives to a two-day offsite to get his staff thinking big and long-term. According to recent study, one of the reasons for the initiative's success was that the administrators and employees engaged firmly believed in the connection between the work they were doing and the goal that motivated it.

Form an instructional design team made up of leaders from all levels and create a framework for discussion and creation of leadership training that senior leaders can utilize to ensure that everyone in the company understands what is essential to them and what is required of them. Give key objectives to the instructional design team that oversees human resources, corporate communications, employee relations, and other departments. This should be included in the whole employee experience, from recruiting to retirement. Empower the instructional design team to lead corporate strategy, program management, operational excellence, and other teams in aligning target setting, investment portfolio management, and other goal-to-results approaches in order to maintain alignment as conditions change.

Design, develop, and implement leadership development programs that are iteratively designed, developed, and deployed by the leaders who engaged in steps one through three above. Iterate material based on the most important aspirations and intents. Leaders must be re-engaged in order to continue their education. Engage learners in refining learning content as the deployment continues by giving application examples, new application scenarios, and hazards. Baseline indicators of employee engagement and sentiment, such as individual experiences with diversity, equity, and inclusion, job value, leadership quality, and teamwork, are used to assess effects. Adaptive Organizations' Leadership Roles When members of the C-suite, talent management, people leaders, and individual contributors (such as subject matter experts) who lead without direct reporting and L&D professionals work together, successful programs emerge.

- They actively participate in the development of leaders by teaching, coaching, and mentoring others.
- They achieve and sustain desired team and individual results.Individuals.
- They take responsibility for your own growth and make use of the resources available to you.
- They look for chances to display, improve, and apply skills. Professionals in learning and development assist trainees in addressing the specific concerns and challenges that leaders face. Integration is preferred over specialization. Combine behavioral and technical skills, as well as do-it-yourself and learn-as-you-go learning. Final Thoughts Transformation must begin inside the CLO, L & D, and other people management professionals if they are to effectively construct adaptable companies.

Incorporate critical thinking, diversity, and other behavioral competencies into the curriculum and learning environment. CLO and L & D professionals add value by empowering and mentoring organization leaders at all levels, regardless of title or tenure. The C-suite adds value by keeping the company's strategy and goals up-to-date and clear. In this new model, CLOs and L & D professionals add value by empowering and mentoring organizational leaders at all levels. Consider the following developing principles to respond to opportunities and disruptions, cross-functional teams must adjust all organizational systems, including incentives and recognition, talent management, and learning and development. Start with your own internal knowledge and skills. When you've found adaptable leaders, search for leadership, technology, and management knowledge from outside sources to continue expanding your adaptive leadership schema. To help you scale, create a leadership team with a single leadership system attitude. Integrate organizational leadership competence and capacity into leaders' daily work flows.

Summing Up

Adaptive businesses have the technical and organizational agility to do so, and workplace settings that support resilience, deeper levels of engagement, and autonomy result in improved performance and employee retention. Instilling learning is another technique to make an organization more adaptive. Culture reflects the habits and attitudes of a company's personnel. A good organizational culture does not happen by chance. A culture that encourages individuals to feel good and motivates them to achieve peak performance motivates them to be extremely successful. Adaptive leaders strike a compromise between their ideal vision of what they want to achieve and the realities of teachers' lives. This intermediate ground is exemplified by the huddle-call structure, which allowed instructors to collaborate on problems but didn't compel them to coordinate their improvement efforts. The Goldilocks zone has the advantage of being long-term and may lead to modest improvements.

CHAPTER SIX

CATALYZE CHANGE

Mobilize Quickly And Empowered To Act

"The measure of intelligence is the ability to change."
— Albert Einstein

Organizations that do so use both hard and soft techniques to bring about change. Individual accountability and metrics are defined, and individuals are given the tools and power they need to succeed in implementation. They keep track of their progress against key milestones, recognize when projects are running late, and take remedial action. In order to preserve trust, they also interact and engage with important stakeholders. Companies frequently make changes to their organization and people aspects in response to external events, hiring more people during good times, laying off employees during bad times, and then offering leadership training when morale eventually drops and the organization experiences whiplash reactions. Others have a more laid-back style with few proactive measures. Neither of these procedures produces consistently good results.

For a long time, no one has endorsed command-and-control leadership. However, no completely defined alternative has arisen. This is largely due to high-level executives' apprehension about changing their own habits. They understand that their organizations must become more innovative, and they believe that this will not happen unless they are ready to delegate control, decision-making, and resource allocation to lower levels of the organization. But they're afraid that if they let go of the reins, the company will implode. An agile organization adjusts swiftly to an ever-changing environment. It is nimble because of three types of leaders. The author investigates leadership capabilities and antecedents to leadership development. Theis section discusses how businesses might evolve from bureaucracy to become more nimble, agile, learning, and networked. A agile organization can swiftly adjust to an ever-changing reality. You used to refer to the world as *"VUCA,"* which stands for *"volatile, uncertain, complex, and ambiguous,"* but now it's a VUCA world on steroids.

Many corporate executives continue to assume that conventional market dominance indicators give an unbeatable competitive edge. However, as the rate of disruption increases, it becomes clear that the largest and *"strongest"* business operators are not always the ones that will survive. As the epidemic has progressed, this has become increasingly obvious, with many firms, large and small, battling to withstand the COVID-19 disruption and its long-term consequences. In ways never seen before, the COVID-19 pandemic has increased the pace of disruption and exposed the degree of globalization and the interconnectedness of technology, business, and society. This transition has also exposed the volatility of individuals formerly regarded as industry leaders.

Not all businesses suffered during the epidemic; in fact, some businesses were fortunate enough to be in the right place at the right time. For example, *"work from home"* businesses and e-commerce giants. Others have managed to stay afloat thanks to a strong emphasis on resilience, financial stability, and contingency preparation. There are, however, some that have strategically leveraged the crisis to develop their company's strategies for growth. In every case, these businesses have proven an exceptional capacity to adapt. The findings of recent survey demonstrate that organizational speed is a critical component of outperformance in times of extraordinary change, and they suggest three approaches for firms to increase speed in the long run. Furthermore, poll results show that putting an extra effort into acquiring speed pays off. Profitability, operational resilience, organizational health, and growth are all areas where fast businesses beat others by a significant margin.

However, increasing speed is not as simple as pressing the accelerator. The negative financial impact of the current crisis on firms has already begun to manifest. Some businesses, particularly those in the travel, hotel, and entertainment industries, have been severely hit and have been forced to take drastic steps to survive, such as layoffs or lowering product or service quality. However, while these moves may be profitable in the near term, they might harm your employer brand and customer happiness in the long run. You are compelled to examine what are doing well and what needs to be improved inside your own organizations.

Now is the moment for businesses to build leaders who can adjust themselves and their organizations to deal with disruptions while doing their daily tasks. Here's how to do it. Adaptive businesses The ability of businesses to adjust to changing circumstances is critical. Disruptions can be viewed as a danger, which requires resistance, or as an opportunity, which requires adaptation. According to the author, the inclusion of *"uncertainty"* in the concept of leadership is a plus since it means that one does not have to know all of the answers. In reality, you can't fix it yourself as a leader in an adaptive environment. All you can do is assist your group in making growth, and that is a success. Taking on a variety of challenges you survive by solving challenges that emerge in the lives of your groups, whether it's an organization, a community, a patient, or an institution.

However, you must consider the nature of the task you are confronted with. Adaptive organizations, according to Deloitte, will succeed. To become an adaptable company, large-scale global enterprises must make a fundamental shift in operating and management philosophy that allows them to function with a start-up mindset and drive current people practices that enable enterprise agility through an empowered network of teams.

Organizations that haven't evolved and adapted sufficiently throughout time those organizations needed a major wakeup call, and they're either going to receive it now or they won't be around, author adds. According to author, this grave prognosis stems in part from the fact that there is no blueprint for this degree of change. . Organizations must develop new methods of working and productivity metrics. Such new ways of working need a level of leadership competency that has not previously been highlighted or rewarded. When faced with a disruption, leaders are put to the test, and they frequently behave in one of two nonproductive ways: Others overconfidently apply unexamined know-how rather than adopting an adaptive approach by defining or reframing issues, exploring new domains, and innovating, rather than taking a reactive approach by defining or reframing problems, exploring new domains, and innovating.

Change is happening at a breakneck speed. Three sorts of leaders help an agile organization adjust fast. The first is the entrepreneurial leaders who come up with innovative goods and business models at a lower level in the organization. They become the organization's innovation engine. There are also enabling leaders who assist entrepreneurial leaders in advancing their ideas and communicating strategic imperatives. Architecting leaders, who are frequently found at the top of an organization, design the game boards on which entrepreneurial and facilitative leaders operate. They enable people to form teams, access resources for fresh ideas, and continue to develop. They also develop funneling systems to strike a balance between inventive freedom and chaos. Interestingly, during the pandemic, pharmaceutical corporations were considerably more agile, forming what you term *"teams of teams."* Most new vaccines and new COVID drugs were developed by corporations that collaborated with regulators, universities, other pharmaceutical companies, and biotech companies. Teams from various organizations were experimenting and breaking down the traditional stages to help propel new goods forward in ways you've never seen before.

The findings of recent survey demonstrate that organizational speed is a critical component of outperformance in times of extraordinary change, and they suggest three approaches for firms to increase speed in the long run. Furthermore, poll results show that putting an extra effort into acquiring speed pays off. Profitability, operational resilience, organizational health, and growth are all areas where fast businesses beat others by a significant margin. However, increasing speed is not as simple as pressing the accelerator. Because of the epidemic, nearly half of those polled said they are reconsidering the type of work they do. Organizations should assess the relationship between their mission and how it is carried out on a daily basis. More clarity about why the company exists should serve as a north star for crucial business decisions, including capital allocation, employee experience, and workforce choices recruiting, reskilling, upskilling programs. Organizations that make a clear connection between what they do and why they exist are more likely to retain employees and customers. As a result, conditions were ideal for large-scale transformation, with companies investing financial and human capital in new or redesigned programs to improve employee experience, productivity, and minimize voluntary turnover to rivals.

Purists and people who believe in a single truth should be avoided by organizations. Purists expect rigid adoption patterns and may reject pathways that are culturally compatible. Purists risk alienating current employees and leaders as well. Between excitement and puritanism, there is no clear distinction. People will be drawn into the cause by enthusiasm, which will foster change from the inside. Forced or regimented change will be met with opposition. Transformation movements with a large number of supporters are more likely to succeed.These vulnerabilities will drive commercial risk and endanger growth and brand without a firm-wide and systematic strategy to organizational resilience.

Is your organization agile?

leaders are increasingly asking themselves and others. It's an essential question, yet answering it is difficult. Because agile has become so popular, many leaders and teams believe they are agile when they aren't. Working with teams and organizations throughout the world, I've seen that agile takes root in different ways in different companies, with four common consequences.

Organizations are described as groups of living entities (people) working toward a common goal. To stay ahead of the competition in an ever-changing and complicated environment, every firm must be hyper-connected to the outside world, continually notice and grab chances, and change itself on a regular basis. Adaptive businesses may align, execute, and refresh themselves more quickly and effectively than their competitors. Rather than *"doing agile"* or *"doing conventional,"* they may work together. They begin by adopting an agile mentality (demonstrating an open and growing attitude) and putting both agile and conventional concepts into practice—being *"stable or efficient"* at the center and *"dynamic or adaptive"* at the periphery.

The negative financial impact of the current crisis on firms has already begun to manifest. Some businesses, particularly those in the travel, hotel, and entertainment industries, have been severely hit and have been forced to take drastic steps to survive, such as layoffs or lowering product or service quality. However, while these moves may be profitable in the near term, they might harm your employer brand and customer happiness in the long run. You are compelled to examine what are doing well and what needs to be improved inside your own organizations.

To support the new activities, changes to organizational structures, roles and duties, processes, procedures, and work instructions will be necessary. To be effective, these changes must be communicated and rolled out in a very controlled and sustainable manner, with implementation assistance for individuals affected and strong change management. Furthermore, travel limitations and supply chain limitations will continue to be significant obstacles in the future. It will be critical to comprehend our clients' changing desires and expectations. To guarantee the optimum fit and alignment with the new customer profiles, business models and value propositions will need to be examined and updated. In these trying circumstances, the slim adage "doing more with less" has never been more applicable. At this critical juncture, organizations will look to their *"Continuous Improvement"* (CI) and quality departments and functions to help lead, drive, and support the organizational change effort; the culture, processes, tools, and support network will be invaluable in successfully navigating the change. Those that have a well-developed CI culture, procedure, and support will undoubtedly have a competitive edge over those who do not.The truth is that most leaders cannot and should not attempt to accomplish everything. The majority of leaders have what I refer to as a leadership signature. This is a unique manner of leadership that encompasses both things they excel at and those they don't. The concept behind the incomplete leader is that no one can be great at everything. Therefore, recognize where you are lacking and what your strengths and weaknesses are. Don't put yourself under the pressure of striving to be flawless. Instead, put together a team of people who can complement your abilities. You may construct a full leader by working together.

The author realized that continuous improvement is not the linear process that many people think it is; rather, it requires a great deal more leadership talent, connection-building, political acumen, judgment, and personal touch. You discovered that both business and health care have understood that continuous improvement strategies do not implement themselves as you read the literature in these fields. Culture-building and leadership of the proper sort are required. At the same time, you discovered that using continuous improvement methodologies in education poses some unique problems.

For good reason, the new management buzzwords are *"agile"* and *"nimble."* The client is king in the new economy. Customer wooing, winning, and retention are important success criteria, and pricing alone is no longer enough. Customer success is crucial because suppliers are responsible not just for product performance but also for the achievement of business value.

Organizations must develop new methods of working and productivity metrics. Such new ways of working need a level of leadership competency that has not previously been highlighted or rewarded. When faced with a disruption, leaders are put to the test, and they frequently behave in one of two nonproductive ways: Others overconfidently apply unexamined know-how rather than adopting an adaptive approach by defining or reframing issues, exploring new domains, and innovating, rather than taking a reactive approach by defining or reframing problems, exploring new domains, and innovating.

All of this necessitates a more agile and flexible business that can make quick, targeted, and adaptable choices and actions in response to constantly changing market dynamics and account conditions. The problem is figuring out how to accomplish it on a large scale. Marketing, customer success, and professional services support operations have grown into enormous enterprises in their own right. Their budgets and headcounts begin here.Their headcounts and budgets begin to match their product development and sales investments. Developing targeted vertical market activities adds another layer to the challenge. To provide maximum value to our customers and stakeholders, you require all of these companies to interact and coordinate as a global corporation. So many interconnected interests, so many stakeholders, and so little time! How is it possible for an elephant to learn to dance?

Agility is difficult for large businesses by definition. Its demands for flexibility, innovation, and the capacity to pivot swiftly in a dynamic environment appear to be at odds with the company's strict structure.However, with the correct structure and cultural mentality, agility on a scale may be achieved. These ten cutting-edge businesses provide proof, demonstrating how others may benefit from agility across the board. Cisco, Barclays, Panera Bread, Ericsson, PlayStation Network, John Deere, Fitbit.

On SBP, Cisco implemented the Scaled Agile Framework (SAFe) and three agile release trains: capabilities, defects and fixes, and projects. The plan was to work together on developing and testing tiny enhancements for a single SaaS component before sending them to the system integration and testing team. Cisco completed the new SBP release on time and without overtime.Thanks to enhanced team cooperation, defects were decreased by 40% and defect elimination efficiency rose by 14% compared to prior waterfall releases. LEGO Digital Solutions is the division of the popular toy-brick manufacturer in charge of consumer contact via computers, applications, wearables, and other platforms. The group began with just five development teams that could readily interact, but as it grew to more than 20 teams, it faced unexpected challenges. The group used the SAFe architecture to build a program level between the teams and the portfolio management process at the top of the business to solve these concerns. As a result, there is less duplication of effort, fewer dependency difficulties, better planning and execution, and more client trust.

When Barclays launched its agile transformation, the financial services firm already had a number of agile teams spread throughout the globe. However, it desired to expand and merge its agile initiatives into a more efficient entity. It went with the learning-oriented Disciplined Agile Delivery strategy, implementing agile coaching and redesigning the company's workspaces to make them more collaborative. More than 800 teams had switched to an agile methodology in less than a year, and Barclay's experienced a 300 percent boost in throughput. Simultaneously, across more than 80 applications, code complexity decreased by 50% on average, while test code coverage improved by 50%. Ericsson's Media Gateway for Mobile Networks (M-MGw) product development was initially organized around component teams and followed a waterfall style. Only a few individuals knew about the product, and organizational silos caused significant lead times and feedback loops. Due to increased competition, the firm used agile and large-scale Scrum (LeSS) to increase flexibility and reduce release cycles. The transformation of M-MGw into a Scrum-based organization began with a few cross-functional pilot teams operating in agile, with the majority of the company remaining in component teams. The firm expanded to more than 15 self-organized teams ahead of its next release as the pilot teams shared their good experiences with others outside those groups.

Organizations must determine how much autonomy, flexibility, and agility their plan requires.

The Group Conventional wisdom says that high-performing individuals are responsible for organizational success. Each team has its own goal or emphasis around which to focus its work and encourage its members; yet, all teams within an organization are eventually linked to the organization's purpose.

Each PlayStation product release necessitates the cooperation of around 1,000 engineers from Sony Interactive Entertainment (SIE) spread across eight cities. However, combining waterfall with Agile Scrum didn't produce satisfactory results since the iteration cycles differed, with various groups iterating daily, weekly, or bi-monthly. SAFe is being used by 700 team members across 60 Scrum teams, and SIE has cut initial planning time by 28% thanks to the framework. The corporation saved around $30 million per year by reducing downtime. Fitbit used Scrum to effectively fulfill its strict customer holiday-driven product release timetable. However, as the firm and its client base developed, it became evident that the company's method would have to be scaled back. Fitbit's program management office director has worked with SAFe before and was instrumental in its implementation. At its first Program Increment (PI) planning session, the organization started with 12 Scrum teams, gradually adding more teams and functional groups with each PI. The organization noticed an improvement in pace and cadence, as well as team engagement, almost immediately. Fitbit produced four new products and sold more than 22 million devices a year after using SAFe, contributing to its successful scaling effort.

The $26 billion medical technology company's time-to-market has a huge influence on millions of people's lives. Royal Philips used a Scrum framework with SAFe principles to replace its conventional development strategy, which took an average of 18 months. The changes were significant. The average release cycle time was cut in half, from 18 to six months, and the feature cycle time was cut in half, from more than 240 days to less than 100. The organization was able to achieve release on demand thanks to consistently on-time sprint and PI delivery. With over 3,700 workers utilizing the SAFe framework, Royal Philips now has more than four agile release trains running across several business areas.

A company that is nimble is one that adapts quickly to changes in the market and workplace trends. Such businesses recognize that organizational change is unavoidable, so they regularly review their practices and processes to ensure that they are conducive to optimal employee engagement, morale, and performance. An agile organization responds to new competitors successfully and quickly; they are innovative and are always challenging themselves to advance, respond, and modify.

In terms of management and outlook, agile organizations have five distinct characteristics that set them apart from more traditional businesses. Agile organizations are more goal-focused, conduct ongoing performance conversations rather than annual performance reviews, and are always looking forward. More specifically, the five characteristics listed below can help you better understand an agile organization. Agile organizations share the same goal and vision. They are adaptable when it comes to resource allocation, and they can recognize and grab opportunities in terms of strategy, giving them a competitive advantage. A flat corporate structure is common in agile organizations. They have hands-on managers, well-defined jobs, and employees who are empowered to achieve their goals. Transparency and on-going learning are priorities for agile organizations. They have a "fail fast" attitude, which means they are willing to try new things. Even if these experiments do not succeed, they provide valuable learning opportunities.Role mobility and entrepreneurial drive are encouraged in agile organizations. Employees that are engaged desire to learn more about the company and assist where they can. Agile businesses promote this way of thinking and acting.Importantly, agile organizations place a high value on efficient, user-friendly technology that facilitates decision-making, communication, and feedback.

Cargill Inc., a food producer and distributor, was unable to engage and motivate its 155,000 global employees prior to its seismic performance management change in 2012. As a result, Cargill made the decision to become a more agile organization, introducing "everyday performance management." This system was built on four pillars, like Continuous feedback is preferable to document-heavy and infrequent feedback. Daily activities and practices are predictors of the quality of performance and management. The relationship between the employee and the manager is crucial. Above all, the system must stay flexible and adaptable in order to satisfy business requirements. It would be unfair to talk about agile performance management without mentioning Adobe, one of the most well-known cases of performance management overhauls. The Adobe team decided to forgo annual performance reviews in favor of regular, on-going performance discussions between managers and employees, which they dubbed "Check-in." Adobe has reduced voluntary turnover by 30% while increasing involuntary departures by 50% since making the change, implying that subpar recruits were being managed more quickly.In addition, the company saved 80,000 management hours each year.

In 2015, General Electric underwent a performance management overhaul, paving the way for other global corporations to follow suit. After years of annual performance reviews and their notorious rank-and-yank performance ratings system (which meant ranking their employees and regularly eliminating the bottom 10%), GE decided they needed to refresh their performance management system.The ranking system was the first to be phased out, although annual assessments lasted another decade. They are now a flexible organization that has made significant progress.

Employees who do best tend to be the most narcissistic and self-promoting, Accenture discovered under its previous system. Accenture wanted to revamp their system and reward employees who made genuine contributions to the company. As a result, they began to incorporate the usage of ongoing performance conversations while refocusing on performance improvement. Forced ranking, according to Accenture, is illogical since it forces employees to compete with coworkers who may have a completely different job. The new system focuses more on the employee and assisting them in becoming the greatest version of themselves possible.

The COVID-19 epidemic has pushed the demand for new worker skills substantially in the last year. The fast expansion of digitalization and remote work has placed new expectations on employees, who, in many cases, now require new abilities to support substantial changes in how work is done and the business goals their firms establish. Also essential is assistance from their employers in developing the skills that will position the company and their people for the future. The importance of solving skill shortages is obvious in the latest McKinsey Global Survey on reskilling—and more essential than ever across industries. Companies have made a substantial shift toward skill training throughout the epidemic, and the need to address skill shortages is more essential than ever. Since the epidemic began, 58 percent of respondents think that addressing skill gaps in their firms' workforces has become a higher priority. And, among the five critical activities to bridge these gaps—hiring, contracting, redeploying, releasing, and developing skills within the present workforce—skill development is more common now than it was before the epidemic. 69% of respondents said their firms are investing more in skill development today than they were before the COVID-19 issue, a substantially larger rise than the other four activities. Empathy, leadership, and flexibility are just a few examples. However, regardless of the skills involved, you discovered that skill transformations, which are large-scale, programmatic efforts to support skill building so that employees can adapt to the fundamentally changing requirements of their current role or move into a new one, have a clear recipe for success. The focus of skill development has been on *"softer"* and *"advanced"* cognitive skills. More than half of respondents said they are focusing on building leadership, critical thinking and decision-making, and project management abilities. When compared to the results from 2019, many of the skills where respondents report the greatest increases in focus fall into two categories: social and emotional skills which account for three of the five largest increases and advanced cognitive skills.

Now is the moment for businesses to build leaders who can adjust themselves and their organizations to deal with disruptions while doing their daily tasks. Here's how to do it. Adaptive businesses The ability of businesses to adjust to changing circumstances is critical. Disruptions can be viewed as a danger, which requires resistance, or as an opportunity, which requires adaptation. According to the author, the inclusion of "uncertainty" in the concept of leadership is a plus since it means that one does not have to know all of the answers. In reality, you can't fix it yourself as a leader in an adaptive environment. All you can do is assist your group in making growth, and that is a success. Taking on a variety of challenges you survive by solving challenges that emerge in the lives of your groups, whether it's an organization, a community, a patient, or an institution. However, you must consider the nature of the task you are confronted with. Adaptive organizations, according to Deloitte, will succeed. To become an adaptable company, large-scale global enterprises must make a fundamental shift in operating and management philosophy that allows them to function with a start-up mindset and drive current people practices that enable enterprise agility through an empowered network of teams. Adaptive leaders are always looking for new methods to match pivotal events with shifting consumer preferences. They are attempting to alter client preferences in ways that benefit both their companies and their customers. They train their employees for both expected and unexpected outcomes. They can feel when things are about to change and react rapidly. These adaptable leaders are able to function effectively, adapt rapidly, invent new methods of working, and alter their businesses in a seamless manner. Organizations must produce leaders who can adjust themselves and their organizations to deal with challenges now.

Entrusting additional decision-making abilities and related resources to staff is one of the techniques these firms use to stay quick and adaptable. Roles are more fluidly defined, according to Hemsley Fraser; the overall strategy may be defined, but the tactics for achieving it remain loose and flexible; decisions are made more quickly because employees are more empowered; the culture is less about judging people and more about encouraging them to be curious; new customer needs and requirements are more likely to be anticipated; agile companies are less afraid to take risks because failing is acceptable; people and organizations are more likely to collaborate; people and organizations are more likely to collaborate According to McKinsey, a company must be both active and stable in order to be agile. Stable procedures nurture stability and efficiency, whereas dynamic practices enable firms to adjust nimbly and promptly to new problems and opportunities. Continuous strategic and financial planning is used by adaptive organizations. When it comes to organizational priorities, there are two speeds. Leaders set the tone, create boundaries, and develop capabilities. In an agile organization, leadership takes on a different form.

Agile leaders play an important role in ensuring alignment on purpose, strategy, and goals. Leaders must express their goals and why they want them, then empower their staff to find out how to get there. The more alignment leaders can achieve, the more autonomy they can provide. (BCG). HR will also have to adapt how work is organized – what should be stable and what should be dynamic, how capability is developed and leveraged, how the organization is led, how design thinking, insights, and data are used, and how the organization responds to ongoing change – all of these factors will have to be considered. Organizations have an urgent need to address changing client needs in a turbulent business environment with aggressive, equally capable rivals now more than ever. As a result, companies are increasingly dealing with more complicated and occasionally chaotic organizational settings, putting their very survival and long-term viability in jeopardy.

As history has repeatedly demonstrated (Kodak, Nokia, and Blockbuster), building an organization's capacity to adapt and prosper over time has become critical. All of these developments will necessitate enhanced openness, cross-functional collaboration, and shared responsibility, as well as significant changes in employment, skills, rewards, and careers. While leaders are supposed to be all-knowing, precisely forecast the future, and be inventive, organizations are plagued with ambiguity, inconsistencies, and contradictions. The evident irony is in how businesses and leaders have viewed challenges: every problem has a solution. The most powerful leaders, on the other hand, recognize that issue resolution is not a *"one-size-fits-all"* activity. They understand that their actions are contingent on the situation, and they make better judgments by adapting their strategy to changing circumstances. Understanding complexity can aid people in better understanding how to act in systems in an organized but non-linear manner. The Cynefin framework is one example of a practical application. Even when things are confusing, many things in life are predictable.

For millennia, science and innovation have helped to make the world more predictable. You can now anticipate the weather, when you will get to our destination (before you leave), and even who will be the best candidate for a job. Companies may even guess what things customers want to buy next in the era of AI and deliver them ahead of time. Humanity appears to value predictability and has made significant investments in it. Despite all of this extraordinary foresight, no one could have imagined that the global spread of a virus would result in such a massive public health and economic disaster in 2020. While some foresaw the possibility of such an occurrence, no one had built the data or tools to spot the early warning signs and respond fast. It's a sharp reminder that the world is still – and probably always will be – unpredictable.Business and organizational leaders must chart a route for the months and years ahead in the light of this volatility. Some industries have witnessed a twofold impact of public health regulations on their personnel and the resulting loss of client demand in recent months, while others have seen a sudden reversal in revenue growth as customers stop their spending plans. Changes in customer behavior have led to an increase in demand in some cases. It's still unclear whether these changes will last, and that uncertainty is simply adding to the fear and caution that many individuals and organizations are displaying in their behavior and decision-making right now.

Summing UP

An agile organization can swiftly adjust to an ever-changing reality. VUCA stands for "volatile, uncertain, complex, and ambiguous". Findings from a recent survey demonstrate that organizational speed is a critical component of outperformance in times of extraordinary change. Increasing speed is not as simple as pressing the accelerator, however. Because of the epidemic, nearly half of those polled said they are reconsidering their job. Organizations should assess the relationship between their mission and how it is carried out on a daily basis. More clarity about why the company exists should serve as a north star for crucial business decisions. A company that is nimble is one that adapts quickly to changes in the market and workplace trends. Agile organizations are more goal-focused, conduct ongoing performance conversations rather than annual performance reviews, and are always looking forward. The COVID-19 epidemic has pushed the demand for new worker skills substantially in the last year. You can't fix it yourself as a leader in an adaptive environment. All you can do is assist your group in making growth, Deloitte says. To become an adaptable company, large-scale global enterprises must make a fundamental shift in operating and management philosophy.

EMBRACING PARADOX

Adjustment Is Required To Accept That No Organization Is Perfect

"Adaptability is not imitation. It means power of resistance and assimilation." -Mahatma Gandhi

Adaptability, according to the author's findings, is a vital success component during times of transformation and systemic change. It enables us to learn more quickly and effectively, and it orients us toward the chances rather than the problems that lie ahead. However, the same circumstances that make adaptation so vital may also cause dread, causing us to fall back on old habits or solutions that worked in the past. The *"adaptability paradox"* describes how, when you most need to learn and change, you remain with what you know, frequently to the detriment of learning and creativity. Even good things, like getting a promotion or starting a new job, can become bad if you don't keep a learning mentality while you're under pressure.

People typically want to cling on to the ideals of their culture that have had personal meaning and relevance for them throughout times of transition. When dominant cultures are confronted with stressors such as immigration, they are forced to review their beliefs and are frequently forced to do extremely difficult integrative work. You stand for freedom and respect for all people, and your policy does not correspond with what you believe in, says the needed leadership.

The refusal of leaders to listen to other people's perspectives is perhaps the biggest obstacle posed by adaptive leadership. Adaptive leadership, as previously said, is more about cooperation than it is about power. Leaders often revert to tried-and-true methods when they require fresh thinking and decisiveness. Five steps can help you flourish in the face of uncertainty by transforming your relationship with it. Shutdowns and supply-chain breaches are common occurrences. Work-from-home, online shopping, and blockchain-based settlements are all possibilities. If it wasn't evident before, the last year has demonstrated that a dynamic and complicated world is throwing up change at a breakneck speed. Individuals and businesses must be prepared. That does not imply that you should respond to the next issue that comes our way, but rather that you should be ready to confront it when it happens. There is one tool in particular that can assist leaders in doing so: flexibility. Adaptability is defined as the ability to learn quickly and effectively in a variety of conditions. It's more of a meta-skill than a skill—learning how to learn and knowing when to put that learner's mind to work. You may keep control over uncertainty by becoming aware of and open to change early, before pressures build to the point when changing direction is considerably more difficult, if not impossible.

People, on the other hand, seldom put in the effort to learn and master anything new unless they have a compelling reason to do so. When motivation strikes, it's frequently accompanied by pressure—pressure to avoid failure, for example, or pressure to achieve a high-stakes reward or incentive. To avoid falling into this trap, leaders must concentrate on changing their attitudes about change and uncertainty by cultivating flexibility as a lifelong talent that helps both themselves and their businesses. Even for the most successful among us, this is not a natural ability, but it can be developed.

Research shows that firms with strong cultures that encourage adaptation do better financially than those that don't. In this book, the author explore five measures that leaders can take to become more flexible, including stressing both well-being and purpose, cultivating an adaptive mindset, deepening human relationships, and creating a safe learning environment. Why is it so crucial to develop an adaptation muscle? During the COVID-19 crisis, the strength of resilience was vividly proved. Although resilience and adaptation are closely related, they differ in key ways.

Leadership Barriers to Adaptive Capacity Changing one's conduct in reaction to adversity does not come easily for many business executives. While most business executives are competent and clever, it can be challenging to acquire new behavioral reactions when their previous habits match their businesses' goals in the majority of circumstances. Introducing new behavioral options is typically unsettling, and it may make leaders feel exposed. People tend to cling to practices that have served them well in the past, which might limit their ability to change. Rather than waiting for agility to spread from the bottom up, HR executives must support and assist leaders in taking command of their transitions. These techniques can aid in the development of an adaptable leadership style.

Organizational silos, unclear strategy, and delayed decision-making, according to the CEOs the author studied, regularly obstruct initiatives to increase work productivity. Building speedier decision-making systems, boosting internal communication and cooperation, and increasing the number of employees are the three main ways that leaders perceive to solve these obstacles. Executives are supervising a seismic shift in how firms function as a result of the pandemic, ranging from tactical changes in areas like meeting format and cadence, and day-to-day management, to enterprise-wide changes in leadership and people management, technology use, and innovation.

As you've seen, organizations are always confronted with technological and adaptive obstacles. Adaptive challenges provide a more unclear problem to be solved, whereas technical challenges have a well-defined problem that can be solved by professionals.

Adaptive leadership as a framework can be a beneficial method to handle such issues. Furthermore, despite the hurdles that come with this strategy, building this skill allows businesses to prosper in the long run. Employees of a phenomenally successful were departing for rivals, despite the fact that they were highly talented and well-trained. Although the firm generated excellent income, staff turnover began to have a negative impact on the bottom line.

There is currently no playbook available to help firms through the present chaos. Many views, as well as thorough measures, are required to present a more realistic picture of contemporary economic challenges. It is more crucial than ever to have leaders that listen and encourage cooperation. Instead of relying on a top-down strategy to maintain the status quo, this unique period requires transformational leadership, in which management collaborates with employees at all levels to implement critical changes. In this new climate, modest executives are more likely to ensure healthy group dynamics and discover the inspiration needed to propel their company ahead. According to McKinsey & Company, modest leaders are more likely to succeed.

Adaptability takes us from enduring a difficulty to thriving beyond it, whereas resilience takes us from surviving a challenge to thriving beyond it. You don't simply "bounce back" from adversity; you *"bounce ahead"* into new realms, learning to be more adaptive as your circumstances change. A multifaceted concept of adaptability includes learning agility, emotional flexibility, and an openness to new experiences. They assist us in maintaining purposeful calm under duress and displaying interest in the face of change. They enable us to respond in ways that are the polar opposite of a knee-jerk reaction by allowing us to make deliberate decisions.

Another significant adaptive problem is finding the correct location, time, and rhythms for cooperation. While those at the top may be enthusiastic about collaborative work, instructors may find that their own preparation time is limited or interrupted by meetings. This issue is exacerbated by the fact that schools and districts prefer to spend their professional development time on one effort after another, thereby risking the ability to engage in one set of goals for an extended period of time.

According to research, adaptability has also been connected to essential psychological abilities such as coping and personal growth. Higher degrees of flexibility in the workplace are linked to increased learning capacity, improved performance, confidence, and creative output. Adaptability is also associated with better levels of social support and general life satisfaction, which are important for psychological and physical well-being. Let's look at five ways leaders may invest in flexibility to prepare for a fast-paced and uncertain future now that you've covered the benefits. Make being happy a habit. Executives have been checking on workers' health since the onset of the COVID-19 outbreak. But it may have been putting the wagon before the horse: a study suggests that leaders suffered from anxiety and burnout symptoms at previously unheard-of levels as they concentrated on others rather than recharging their own batteries. In the fall of 2020, a Harvard Business Review–sponsored poll garnered comments from over 1,500 respondents from 46 countries, the majority of whom were at or above the supervisor level. 85% claimed their well-being had deteriorated, while 56% said their job obligations had worsened. Furthermore, 62% of those who were having trouble managing their workloads stated they had burned out *"often"* or *"very frequently"* in the preceding three months. Since then, the number of workers experiencing higher burnout symptoms has risen across the board, not only in C-suites. CEOs are afraid that their leaders will be unprepared to deal with expected challenges. They also desire greater results from their leadership development efforts. That entails creating adaptive leadership skills and providing them at an organizational level for the chief learning officer (CLO) and learning and development (L & D) professionals.

People who are weary have a scarcity mindset (they focus on what they don't have) and are less adaptive and receptive to learning. These mental-health and well-being issues are likely to persist for at least the next year or two.The greatest method for dealing with difficult conditions is to first invest in one's own well-being. Leaders must be healthy to confront whatever comes their way and to assist others for as long as it takes, just like athletes who invest in their physical and mental health on a regular basis, not just before a game or a race. Leaders should prioritize enabling themselves to grow before assisting others in reaching their full physical, mental, and emotional potential.

Another research found that persons who took breaks to mentally reset improved far more quickly under pressure when doing a job that required new abilities. Attending to one's own physical well-being is not selfish, contrary to what some leaders believe. Rather, good physical and mental health are required to develop strong decision-making abilities in the face of ambiguity. Many executives believe they must demonstrate to their organizations that they are constantly on, never being away of the office for lengthy periods of time or taking necessary vacations. One adversary of the adaptable mentality for leaders is the assumption that it is their role to know when to ask the correct questions rather than having the *"perfect answers."* It's essentially the same trap that Zen Buddhism warns about, advising practitioners to adopt what it calls shoshin, or beginner's mentality. According to this notion there are numerous possibilities in the beginner's mind. There aren't many, in the expert's opinion. What you now know is that this beginner's mind is a learnable talent for everyone, not a fixed personality attribute or a skill reserved for Zen masters. You can develop yours by putting forth the effort. Leaders who relinquish their expert status might better manage unpredictable situations by gathering data in novel and effective ways. Leaders may demonstrate flexibility in finding answers by adjusting their mentality to foster learning, curiosity, and willingness to change.

For example, when burnout rates climbed, C-suite leaders of a global firm struggled with how to effectively support employees during the epidemic. The CEO, as a follower of the *"expert attitude,"* believed he should already know the answers and couldn't tolerate the ambiguity. He was advised to address the situation from several angles, such as enlisting the help of team members with nursing, military, and paramedic backgrounds who have dealt with trauma before. Awareness of your default thoughts, knowing when they aren't benefiting you, opening up to what else could be true, and consciously moving into new, flexible thinking are all necessary steps in such a journey. Adaptability relies heavily on self-awareness and reflection. Making a to be list—that is, a list of the values You wish to embody—and setting your intentions in the morning, before a hectic day, or at work when things get hard, are two ways to enhance awareness. Reflecting about challenging times at the end of the day aids in the development of a flexible unlocking mentality for the future. The essential problem is not whether you experience fear or uncertainty—you will—but whether you respond to those pressures in ways that cause us to do more of the same instead of learning and changing.

Increase the variety and depth of your connections. Human beings require meaningful connections to survive and develop; therefore, strong interpersonal interactions help them adapt. According to studies, these social networks can have an impact on one's lifespan. You normally go about your everyday work routines, actively doing things and indirectly collaborating with coworkers to complete those tasks. But that emphasis is misplaced: failing to pay attention to colleagues is really harmful to your health and productivity at work. Deep and diversified social ties that give social support, according to research, are essential aspects of the complex tapestry that feeds your well-being and learning, especially during times of uncertainty and heightened stress.

There are a few things you can do as a leader to help people form stronger bonds: Concentrate entirely on the person in front of you. You frequently allow your attention to wander during conversations, or you multitask by checking our phone or email. Tuning your consciousness toward the other person and listening carefully and without judgment is required for full attention. People can hear you when they feel heard. Be willing to be vulnerable.

Bring your true self to the table and be open to expressing your worries, anxieties, and flaws. While being exposed might seem dangerous, it is always a conscious decision.Empathy is important, but don't stop there. Empathy is insufficient on its own. Leaders may learn to harness the correct type of empathy, which entails considering the other person's point of view without becoming distracted from the matter at hand or, perhaps, wasting their own energy on negative emotions. Once you've grasped the other person's viewpoint, you'll be able to choose the best course of action. Approach others with empathy. If you see someone else's distress, whether physical, emotional, or social, show that you want to help. Simultaneously, bear in mind that you'll never entirely comprehend what they're going through, so have an open mind. While random acts of kindness are appreciated, compassion is more subtle and tailored to an individual's needs. Adaptability is aided by positive team dynamics. Working in groups has an impact on how you prioritize learning, particularly from setbacks and mistakes.

The lack of confrontation and the appearance of conformity, on the other hand, may not represent that dynamic. Teams can have cultures in which setbacks and failures are ignored or, worse, penalized, or cultures in which setbacks are viewed as chances to learn and improve. Leaders may have a significant impact on the team culture that is established based on how well they nurture psychological safety. This is a team-wide notion that taking interpersonal risks is safe—that ideas, questions, worries, and blunders will be embraced and encouraged. Experiencing safety is a necessary component of enhanced performance, creativity, and well-being. It encourages everyone to participate fully and authentically, promotes healthy discussion and innovative problem solutions, and helps teams to learn rapidly. Leaders must be aware of and model the required behaviors, as well as intentionally assist team members, for such an environment to succeed. Simply put, by establishing psychological safety, leaders demonstrate their own adaptability while also fostering an atmosphere in which their people may thrive. This is in stark contrast to a leader who feels, *"I am the best"*, and the team should follow me. The new CEO chose to embark on a journey with this team in order to turn that difficult past into a tale of optimism and opportunity. He enlisted the support of outside coaches to promote team learning, feedback, curiosity, and transformational attitudes. Despite hiccups in the path, the group evolved from a collection of individuals lacking mutual trust to a close-knit team that is much stronger today. Because of the CEO's focus on creating trust, as well as his development mentality and willingness to look vulnerable, a new culture of psychological safety was able to emerge. There are four strategies to increase scaled adaptability.

As practice, use bite-size training. Deeper awareness and habit-shifting work were thought to be only possible through intensive in-person interactions, according to popular thinking. The COVID-19 pandemic, like so many other paradigms, shifted that viewpoint. Many companies have implemented brief digital training courses along with behavioral-reinforcement techniques like nudges. This material focuses on teaching fundamental adaptation ideas that participants may apply in their daily lives to help them learn and modify their behaviors more quickly. This method has proven to be beneficial to businesses in transition, such as a worldwide corporation that underwent a difficult merger before the pandemic struck. It created a wholly digital program to teach 5,000 of its top people managers to increase their flexibility. The program consisted of a dozen 20- to 30-minute lessons delivered over the course of three months, with weekly emails to promote adaptive practices. Participants who engaged with the majority of the content (four to six hours over three months) showed 2.7 times the improvement in adaptability behaviors (learning skills, empathy and compassion, and fostering psychological safety and greater self-awareness) and 3 times the improvement in outcomes (performance, well-being, adapting to change, and developing new skills) as the control group.

A terrible example of leadership that adapts the author has dealt with several leaders who are adamant about not second-guessing their own actions. After some time has passed, you should revisit your choice since circumstances and the rationale for it might have changed. Just because you said no to trying a new product last year doesn't imply you shouldn't try it again this year. His experience has shown that dogmatism and reputation frequently get in the way of leaders. All you have to do now is make sure you don't fall into the same mistake again. When some of the change's prerequisites changed, you reviewed the software several times. This isn't to say you always halted the change, but at the very least the boundaries of the choice were reassessed, and a decision to proceed or to stop or adjust the approach was made. This procedure had little to no status attached to it, which the author believes was crucial. This leader was prepared to revise his own decisions if necessary, not believing that doing so would be a sign of surrender or loss, or even incompetence. Adaptive leaders, in principle, should be open to listening to and modifying suggestions made by coworkers or clients.

Using everyone's abilities rather than simply those of top-level leaders is what an ideal talent mix includes. A clear charter ensures that the organization or team adheres to well-defined goals, responsibilities, and ground rules, while trust fosters strong links between employees, employers, and other stakeholders. Consider how many top executives have crashed and burned in recent years, sometimes after long periods of considerable success. Consider colleagues you've worked with in less visible roles, such as those in charge of major transformation efforts in their businesses who have unexpectedly lost their jobs. Consider this: Have you ever been pulled or pushed aside when practicing leadership? Being a leader entails taking risks. While leadership is frequently portrayed as an exciting and glamorous pursuit in which you encourage people to follow you through good and terrible times, this image overlooks leadership's dark side: the inevitable attempts to remove you from the game.

There are two barriers preventing businesses from responding to new circumstances. Hierarchical arrangements, for starters, stifle team effectiveness by reducing decision-making and communication. Second, most team leaders are actually process managers who are at ease when it comes to technical operations but uncomfortable when it comes to disturbances. They attempt to apply operational abilities to adaptive obstacles, but instead of generating fresh solutions, they resort to patching problems. Leaders must leave their comfort zones and take on adaptive problems with no obvious answers in order to prepare for the future.

Most top executives are hesitant to abandon long-standing rules that helped their firms get off the ground. Sticking to old habits, on the other hand, might prevent you from reaping the benefits of new tactics. People in positions of power are frequently forced to pay the price for a weak plan or a string of poor judgments. But, more often than not, something else is at work. You're not talking about office politics here; you're talking about the high-stakes dangers you confront while leading a company through a difficult but essential transformation. Change that actually transforms an organization, whether it is a multibillion-dollar corporation or a ten-person sales team, necessitates individuals giving up things they hold dear: daily habits, loyalties, and ways of thinking.Developing a shared goal like this necessitates a high level of leadership ability. Finding something that fits teachers' perceived needs, is compatible with the expectations of the external world, and advances the improvement agenda ahead is the skill of determining the focus of an endeavor. Sometimes the purpose emerges from the needs of teachers and schools; in this case, the leader's responsibility is to listen and distill some shared aims, much like a community organizer might. The motivation might come from anywhere. For example, you looked at a foundation-supported early-literacy campaign and a biology initiative that sprang out of university research.

Establish a Common Goal Any leader's first and most crucial responsibility is to establish a shared purpose for the work. Because it cannot be mandated, this is a leadership duty. You can have everyone do the same thing, but only if there is a shared desire to achieve a similar goal have you built a collective purpose. Thus, in the schooling setting, where instructors operate in loosely tied organizations, privacy norms exist, and visions of excellent teaching differ greatly, the very first stage of any continuous improvement process—finding a shared problem to focus on—is more challenging than it appears. These components can be combined to create a whole that is greater than the sum of its parts. Developing a shared goal generates energy and guarantees that everyone is rowing in the same direction. Educators' capacity to engage in reflective practice is used to develop dispositions, which allows individuals participating in the process to change them to match the demands of their setting. By shielding this activity from competing priorities, it can take root and grow over time. All of this needs strong leadership and close attention. Even the most obviously reasonable approach, continuous improvement, turns out to need highly experienced adaptive leadership to attain its goals.

The current crisis serves as a stark reminder that firms are continuously confronted with developments that endanger their bottom line, some minor and some severe. Being agile, adaptable, and resilient can help you address these difficulties when they arise, with the least amount of disruption to your organization. It's fair to say that 2020 hasn't exactly ushered in the new decade in the manner that many had hoped. Despite the uncertainty and upheaval, I believe that this atmosphere of constant change will be the stimulus for business leaders to ultimately reform their operations in order to survive in the digital age. Business executives throughout the world are now confronted with a harsher reality regarding the haste with which digital transformation must occur.

Summing Up

Adaptability is defined as the ability to learn quickly and effectively in a variety of conditions. It's more of a meta-skill than a skill—learning how to learn and knowing when to put that learner's mind to work. The *"adaptability paradox"* describes how, when you most need to learn and change, you remain with what you know.

Research shows that firms with strong cultures that encourage adaptation do better financially. Adaptability relies heavily on self-awareness and reflection. Leaders who relinquish their expert status might better manage unpredictable situations. Reflecting about challenging times at the end of the day aids in the development of a flexible unlocking mentality. A leader should be open to listening to and modifying suggestions made by coworkers or clients. A clear charter ensures that the organization or team adheres to well-defined goals, responsibilities, and ground rules. Using everyone's abilities rather than just those of top-level leaders is what an ideal talent mix includes. Developing a shared goal generates energy and guarantees that everyone is rowing in the same direction. All of this needs strong leadership and close attention from all levels of the organization.

CHAPTER EIGHT

WORKPLACE MANAGEMENT

Embrace A Philosophy That Encourages Real-Time Collaboration And Participation

"None of us, including me, ever do great things. But we can all do small things, with great love, and together we can do something wonderful." – Mother Teresa

You are enthusiastic about empowering individuals and organizations to thrive in the face of continual and disruptive change, and you accomplish this via programs that address organizational change, resilience, agility, leadership, transformation, and adaptation. Strong organizations are what make the difference for successful businesses.

How can you create a healthy workplace?

Make sure you have a coherent leadership team, that the leadership team has a common purpose, that you overcommunicate that objective to all employees, and that you reinforce it in all human processes. This ushered in a new age for business, one in which the ability to adapt is crucial to existence. Leaders must analyze their behaviors and how they effect their companies as part of adaptive leadership training.

HR can ensure that leaders learn from the past, adapt to the present, and prepare for the future by effectively transforming and demonstrating adaptive capacity. For the development of adaptive leadership a new leadership development framework is required. One that can be given at scale and creates adaptable leaders at all levels, sooner in their careers and in the flow of their work. The new model stresses learning in the context of the organization's business conditions, processes, and objectives, as well as quick implementation of what has been learned. Starting with helping leaders understand the business, including its goals, mission, and goods and services, there are six activities and numerous keys to producing adaptable leaders.

Form an instructional design team made up of leaders from all levels and create a framework for discussion and creation of leadership training that senior leaders can utilize to ensure that everyone in the company understands what is essential to them and what is required of them. Give key objectives to the instructional design team that oversees human resources, corporate communications, employee relations, and other departments. This should be included in the whole employee experience, from recruiting to retirement. Empower the instructional design team to lead corporate strategy, program management, operational excellence, and other teams in aligning target setting, investment portfolio management, and other goal-to-results approaches in order to maintain alignment as conditions change. Form an instructional design team made up of leaders from all levels and create a framework for discussion and creation of leadership training that senior leaders can utilize to ensure that everyone in the company understands what is essential to them and what is required of them. Give key objectives to the instructional design team that oversees human resources, corporate communications, employee relations, and other departments. This should be included in the whole employee experience, from recruiting to retirement. Empower the instructional design team to lead corporate strategy, program management, operational excellence, and other teams in aligning target setting, investment portfolio management, and other goal-to-results approaches in order to maintain alignment as conditions change.

Employees have a say in where they work, shaping the dialogue, shaping the workplace, and eventually impacting leadership choices, which is a key part of adaptable workplaces. Employees' well-being, passion for the job, and dedication to the firm are all enhanced when they have a sense of choice and control over when, how, and where they conduct their work. Here are a few instances of workplaces that are adaptable: Siemens has stated that its workers would be able to work two or three days a week from wherever they feel most productive. Employees at Twitter may work from anywhere in the world at any time. With no top-down-driven minimum need for in-office work, most professionals and project teams at Deloitte establish the adaptable working environment that works best for them and their clients.

Improved work/life balance and reduced stress: reports of reduced stress and burnout, as well as increased productivity and more time to focus on family support, as a result of the ability to telework or work remotely, even for one or two days per week. Using everyone's abilities rather than simply those of top-level leaders is what an ideal talent mix includes. A clear charter ensures that the organization or team adheres to well-defined goals, responsibilities, and ground rules, while trust fosters strong links between workers, employers, and clients.

According to a Gartner poll of more than 800 HR professionals, nine HR trends have emerged as a long-term effect of the workforce and workplace changes caused by the coronavirus pandemic disruption. For those executives, the task now is to examine the impact of each HR trend on their organization's operations and strategic goals, determine which demands immediate action. As a cost-cutting tactic, 32% of companies are replacing full-time staff with contingent labor.

Executives C-Suite Calculate and plot business outcomes on a timeline. Describe the technical and interpersonal skills you've developed as a result of your leadership development. Ensure that articulated purpose and talent management executives are enabled by competences. Explain the stages of leadership competency for different types of leaders, such as individual contributors, subject matter experts, project managers, executives, people leaders, high performers, and emerging executives.Incorporate expected outcome delivery into recruiting, onboarding, learning and development, and performance management methods. Ensure that thought leaders' leadership approaches are tailored to your organization's goals.

Design, develop, and implement leadership development programs that are iteratively designed, developed, and deployed by the leaders who engaged in steps one through three above. Iterate material based on the most important aspirations and intents. Leaders must be re-engaged in order to continue their education. Engage learners in refining learning content as the deployment continues by giving application examples, new application scenarios, and hazards. Baseline indicators of employee engagement and sentiment, such as individual experiences with diversity, equity, and inclusion, job value, leadership quality, and teamwork, are used to assess effects. Adaptive organizations' leadership Roles when members of the C-suite, talent management, people leaders, and individual contributors (such as subject matter experts) who lead without direct reporting and L&D professionals work together, successful programs emerge.

Thoughts of transformation must begin inside the CLO, L & D, and other people management professionals if they are to effectively construct adaptable companies. Consider the following developing principles: To respond to opportunities and disruptions, cross-functional teams must adjust all organizational systems, including incentives and recognition, talent management, and learning and development. Start with your own internal knowledge and skills. When you've found adaptable leaders, search for leadership, technology, and management knowledge from outside sources to continue expanding your adaptive leadership schema. To help you scale, create a leadership team with a single leadership system attitude. Integrate organizational leadership competence and capacity into leaders' daily work flows. Incorporate critical thinking, diversity, and other behavioral competencies into the curriculum and learning environment. CLO and L & D professionals add value by empowering and mentoring organization leaders at all levels, regardless of title or tenure. The C-suite adds value by keeping the company's strategy and goals up-to-date and clear. In this new model, CLOs and L & D professionals add value by empowering and mentoring organizational leaders at all levels.

Adaptive ability will continue to determine who emerges on top and who goes away in 2022. HR executives can assist corporate leaders in evaluating their default habits and embracing their ability to adjust. The Impact of the Pandemic on Businesses The epidemic shook up the corporate world, especially in terms of how people see leadership, delegation, performance management, and trust. It also prompted concerns regarding remote work productivity, procedures that obstruct existing processes, new health and safety-related job standards, and how to benefit from new production and delivery methods. The ability of businesses to respond to these issues is strongly tied to their executives' ability to adapt.

Many firms managed to modify their operations models throughout the pandemic, according to McKinsey & Co., with the development of remote work. Businesses that had a successful transformation were more likely to perform in the top quartile of their peers. Businesses that did not invest in change, on the other hand, fared the poorest. This just goes to demonstrate that adaptability is the key to future success. It's vital to remember that adaptive capability is a continuum. Some leaders (and organizations) are considered inherently nimble, while others must work hard to improve their adaptability. However, in the long term, the efforts to overcome any barriers will be worthwhile. All HR executives need to do now is get the rest of the firm on the same page.

HR executives must explain why agility and flexibility are so important for success, and leaders must recognize the need of adaptive capability leadership. Then, and only then, should executives be encouraged to think about the company's operational model. Is it assisting and connecting teams rather than hindering them? Is it going to pave the road for a prosperous future? Finally, HR professionals should collaborate with corporate leaders to guarantee that the transition takes fewer than 18 months to accomplish. This, according to McKinsey & Co., will maintain momentum and prevent the organization from becoming exhausted. One of the first duties for anybody trying to design a learning path for teachers is to make sure that the task's scope is appropriate for the amount of time and other resources required to complete it. More disruptive changes, according to HR experts, will backfire.

The problem is frequently unknown or difficult to define; it is linked to underlying patterns or dynamics and necessitates learning. The remedy is also unknown, necessitating learning. Those who are affected by the challenge (stakeholders), including authorities, have responsibility. The barriers are more intangible: hearts and minds, ideals, loyalty, and connections. Adaptive difficulties are the most difficult because leadership techniques

Author has made it a point to focus on onboarding processes for new recruits, many of whom will work remotely due to spread teams and limited in-person connection chances. This entails establishing mentorship, shadowing, and relationship-building opportunities, as well as information transfer and training. Author frequently attends virtual onboarding sessions and conducts virtual coffee talks with new recruits and other executives. In a virtual setting, these are more viable and easy to arrange. Author interacts with his colleagues early and regularly on objectives and initiatives, despite having limited in-person contact with them. Virtual collaboration tools, shared documents, project-tracking tools, and knowledge libraries enable real-time transparency and documentation, ensuring that everyone in the team is up-to-date at all times. Author connects with people on a regular basis through short one-on-one check-ins. Author has noticed a significant boost in her team's performance as well as increased employee happiness after switching to a hybrid approach.

Author uses a *"little and often"* approach to virtual communication with families, such as short phone calls or text updates, to help her establish connections in preparation for longer visits and more intensive chats. Improved interaction with teenagers and young people: According to anecdotal evidence, virtual communication channels are especially effective with teenagers and young people. Author notices that teens are more engaged, probably because they are more at ease in their own space and are used to interacting with their friends and classmates via text and video chats.

To make work easier for everyone, author's team agreed on which tasks should be done collectively and which should be done separately. The team, for example, decided that planning activities should be done jointly but that targeted activities, such as data analysis, should be done alone. Juan might organize collaborative activities on their team's co-located days by doing this for a variety of projects. Making virtual watercoolers a possibility: While there is no alternative to face-to-face conversations, there are techniques to replicate comparable, spontaneous encounters in a virtual environment. Juan and his colleagues use a range of channels to enable seamless collaboration between co-located and remote workers.

The author and a few members of his team, similar to friends who study or work out together, may occasionally connect to a videoconference connection while working on their individual tasks, often in complete silence. This allows author and his coworkers to concentrate on their own tasks while still allowing for spontaneous dialogue and cooperation. Author hosts open and fully optional office hours for his staff once a week, during which anyone is welcome to come in and speak. The goal is to avoid having an agenda and instead foster unstructured dialogues in which participants may express their thoughts, comments, and anything else on their minds. Author's team makes use of chat tools to encourage casual conversation and information exchange over the internet. Because of virtual working arrangements, team have been able to employ qualified people from all across the country without regard to geography.

Consider yourself the HR Director of a corporation with a significant turnover rate. Employees that are highly trained and competent are leaving the company for rivals, which has a negative impact on the bottom line. What strategy would you use to tackle this problem?If you approach this scenario as a technological problem, you could be inclined to use technical solutions to fix it. Perhaps you require a new incentive scheme to keep your top employees? Perhaps they require more frequent rewards? Perhaps their bosses aren't doing a good job encouraging and engaging them, and they need to improve? You could attempt these remedies and discover that they either don't work or just work for a short period of time. An adaptive lens may be more successful in solving this problem in the long run. If you think this is an adaptive difficulty, you should spend some time investigating what's going on. The alternative is to lose individuals and miss out on important talent. Employment flexibility 44% was cited as the primary reason for people who briefly left the workforce returning. The importance of flexibility is obvious, and leaders should think about these three aspects of flexibility if they truly want to meet their employees' needs.

HR Analytics provides answers to crucial questions about the people who work for the company, allowing them to develop more robust systems for recruiting, productivity, pay, and retention. The following picture shows the essential questions. HR analytics benefits firms by assisting them in making proactive decisions that help them mitigate risks and stay on top of things. It may assist in the provision of vital data and the subsequent improvement of spending, productivity, and operations, all of which benefit a business holistically. Reassuring staff that analytics enhances human decision-making, helps preserve rigor, and keeps initiatives focused on addressing business problems is one way firms may overcome the hurdles of embracing HR analytics. In the long run, the objective is to improve the HR function's analytical abilities and enable HR to better manage the workforce's future. This is the pressing need of the hour.

According to LinkedIn research, 93 percent of Indian organizations intend to fill available positions internally in the post-Covid era. Internal mobility, data-driven recruiting choices, and increasing employee experience are all emerging themes. According to LinkedIn's Future of Talent research, in the post-covid age, more than 9 out of 10 (93%) Indian organizations are trying to fill available positions internally. The inaugural edition of the *"Future of Talent"* study, published by the professional networking platform, looked at the changing role of HR in India as well as how talent is acquired, engaged with, and developed in the current business climate. According to the research, companies are increasingly opting to fill positions internally.

The research also emphasizes the rising emphasis on upskilling, which will be a key component of firms' future workforce strategies. According to the research, 95% of Indian organizations have dedicated L & D programs to assist employees learn new skills and prepare for the future. Other developing trends, such as internal mobility, data-driven recruiting choices, and increasing employee experience, will be on businesses' minds in 2021. According to the survey, 91% of Indian organizations utilize data to make educated talent-hiring decisions, and 53% use data to map capabilities to open job criteria. Furthermore, 9 out of 10 businesses are consolidating positions to save money on recruiting and make remote hiring more effective.

According to Gartner, organizations will continue to expand their use of contingent workers post-COVID-19 in order to maintain more flexibility in workforce management, and they will consider introducing other job models seen during the pandemic, such as talent sharing and 80% pay for 80% work.

According to McKinsey & Company, modest leaders exhibit *"intentional calm,"* which helps them to disconnect from the circumstance and think more clearly about how to handle it. During times of transition, stability is both a struggle and a must. Businesses need to offer even more security to employees and customers, who are already stressed by big lifestyle changes. This is best accomplished through a solid and resilient corporate culture, which may help firms stay on track even when they embark on ambitious projects or face crises.The most successful firms used a combination of proactive and reactive components to develop an agility-resilience framework, according to data collected from 325 enterprises. The study found that firms with more agility-resilience had higher returns on investment and equity. As a result, more stability can aid adaptability and company survival during periods of rapid change. Even before the pandemic, a research published in Consulting Psychology Journal: Practice and Research in 2019 showed the unique interaction between stability and resilience. According to data collected from 325 firms, the most successful companies used a combination of strategies.

An adaptive company is always better suited to meet difficulties and deal with adversity. People in such settings are more resilient and have a renewed willingness to face challenges. They are more capable of drifting through problems quickly as a consequence of their grit. Accepting failure is the first step in becoming more adaptive. Accepting failure is not the same as giving up or quitting. Accepting setbacks as a transient situation is to invite failure. A stepping stone to knowledge. It's all about seizing opportunities to advance. Accepting different ideas from various people in business is one way to build a culture that is receptive to failure. Having a pulse on weather change energises consumers and provides incentives for trying out new products or services. It is critical for everyone to understand their role in delivering value to make a company adaptive. Every member of the team is responsible for ensuring the organization's success. Everyone must take the initiative and behave as a leader. Organizations must accept new ideas and make adjustments as a result. It is best to engage new minds and take advantage of their recent learning to ensure an influx of ideas. Employees must also be taught how to think and act strategically.

A mission that is obvious and unmistakable, presented as a simple "big concept" that all employees can connect to and are pleased to communicate with friends and coworkers. An atmosphere of shared responsibility for the organization's future success, in which all employees are encouraged to think independently, be sensitive to one another, be kind and supportive of one another, and behave with humanity. Adaptability is essential for a company's ability to respond successfully to changing business conditions. Almost every company prepares how to function when business conditions are predictable, but the key to long-term survival is being able to adapt successfully to the unexpected. The mission statement is important because it informs you what to focus on and what to focus on doing. It is simply the measures you take on a regular basis to achieve your objective.

As a result, vision and mission must be in sync. Missions, like visions, should be clear, succinct, and easy to understand. After all, they are guidelines on how everyone in the company should focus their efforts.Surprisingly, the study of business objectives is hampered by a lack of unanimity and clarity about what constitutes a strong purpose. So the author is here to inform you that a strong mission statement must have the following elements: As an adaptable leader, you must assist all members of your business in identifying the fundamental mission guidelines that collectively lead to the vision you all desire. A mission must be quantifiable as well. This is necessary so that leadership can regularly analyse the extent to which your mission's work activities are contributing to the achievement of your vision. Furthermore, good missions do not exist in frames and webpages. They exist in the hearts and minds of everyone in your organization. How probable is it that if you strolled around your building and randomly questioned 10 workers from different levels of your business, they would be able to recite and describe your purpose without having to look it up? If they are unable to describe your mission, you don't have one.

The structure is progressive. High-performance businesses are adaptable, sensing market shifts and making strategic adjustments on the fly. The broad strokes of traditional strategy are supplemented rather than replaced by this approach. They provide their firms' peripheries—far from the traditional strategy function—the authority to act in response to market changes. Furthermore, successful companies regularly monitor and measure their adherence to these traits with the same zeal and expertise they demand of themselves in terms of financial and operational performance. The search for the optimal organizational and human traits is no longer a black box. Just as the introduction of MRI technology gave doctors a previously inaccessible visual depiction of organs and muscles, this framework provides businesses a window into previously unknown internal dynamics, and access to this information may lead to sustained performance. The idea is that the organization would reach peak performance through improving the psychological well-being of its employees. As a result, the culture must contain triggers that cause people to act in specific ways and feel accountable for the company's future success. Purpose, vision, cultural values, business values, and architecture are the key causes.

The ability to constantly analyze all relevant information in order to adjust to current impacts is critical for business agility. If not, can you make them more relevant by transforming them? All too frequently, executives devote valuable effort to developing risk management and business continuity strategies only to realize that their firms are unprepared to deal with an environment that is more volatile and uncertain than ever before. Organizational Resilience—an organization's capacity to foresee, plan for, respond to, and adapt to gradual change and unexpected shocks in order to survive and thrive—is the answer. Resilience is a long-term and often insurmountable problem. Organizations in every industry are continuously tested and stretched by slow-growing disruptions as well as shocks and disasters. The repercussions of operational failures in a more connected society have been highlighted by recent high-profile blunders, accidents, and tragedies. Organizations sleepwalk into failure due to complex and sometimes unnoticed systemic organizational flaws and cultural difficulties.

The creation of answers to these resilience issues is as much a leadership and organizational challenge as it is a scientific and technological undertaking. In many respects, the adaptability required over a longer period of time as the context, product or service needs in the industry change is even more challenging. Following the status quo, which has worked successfully in the past, may result in success progressively fading when new businesses emerge with new operational models or services. This sort of adjustment requirement might be subtle, only becoming obvious when it is too late. Organizations must be receptive to the idea of future-proofing their processes and products. Organizational resilience entails not just avoiding or responding to negative occurrences, but also 'shifting before the cost of not changing becomes too high,' utilizing opportunities, and pushing innovation in order to be competitive in the face of adversity. Organizations must be receptive to the idea of future-proofing their processes and products. Organizational resilience entails not just avoiding or responding to negative occurrences, but also 'shifting before the cost of not changing becomes too high,' utilizing opportunities, and pushing innovation in order to be competitive in the face of adversity. It's not always easy to see the broad picture, handle change, and succeed without stumbling over what's directly in front of you.

In the long run, an adaptive lens may be more successful in solving this problem. If you think this is an adaptive difficulty, you should spend some time investigating what's going on. You might enlist the help of your HR department or engage an outside expert to do an objective evaluation of what is pushing your staff to go. It's possible that the issue isn't with the wage structure or the incentive system, but with the overall culture of the company. In most teams, there is a general lack of responsibility, and employees blame one another for not meeting deliverables. Further investigation may reveal that the organization's leadership team, which includes you, is just as much a part of the equation as you are.

High-performance companies have clearly defined responsibilities that are meticulously put together to make a highly efficient company. People are aware of what is expected of them and which decisions they have control over. Employees understand when and with whom they must cooperate when accountability is shared. Role charters are one way we help firms achieve this clarity, but the name is less essential than having a route to explicit accountability, decision rights, and behavioral requirements. Clear roles eliminate the uncertainty that hinders decision-making and boost modern businesses' performance potential and employee engagement. Peers in a company can use role charters to have open and honest discussions about individual, collective, and shared responsibilities.

While many businesses excel in recruitment, training, or performance management, high-performance firms excel at translating their company plan into a compelling people strategy. HR serves as a key advisor to business units on both operational and strategic people concerns in these businesses. It includes short- and long-term strategies for attracting, developing, and keeping the best individuals with the best skills.

A key asset is the employer brand. Employer brands are well-defined in high-performance firms. Employees and recruits alike are aware of the wide variety of perks available to them, including professional growth, job rotation, and prestige, as well as flexibility and autonomy. This brand—or employee value proposition—contributes to a company's competitive advantage and strengths. Employee development is prioritized in high-performance firms, which invest in training and rotation of jobs and responsibilities. These encounters may beat remuneration and other financial incentives as a significant motivator and retention strategy. They also promote teamwork and decrease the chances of localized leadership. By the time they reach the upper echelons, employees have a comprehensive view of the company.

Talent management is a far larger function than most businesses believe. It isn't just for those who are on the fast track. It also addresses the people and jobs that are crucial to a company's success. Relationship managers in financial brokerages and diagnostic testers in medical laboratories, for example, must be considered as valuable employees, even if they will never be in positions of leadership. These important jobs and people are identified by high-performance businesses, which then center retention tactics and contingency plans around them. This list of people and jobs should be fluid, altering in response to the firm's strategic goals. The management of bad performers is the polar opposite of talent management. The way a company manages the development or departure of low-performing individuals sends a strong message to the rest of the company about what will be tolerated and praised. HR is a strategic partner and a business enabler. People strategy is as important as business strategy in leading firms.

People strategy is as important as business strategy in leading firms. Through people initiatives, the HR department has successfully transformed business strategy into people objectives and supported business priorities. Strategic, functional, and transactional activities are clearly separated within the function. It effectively completes functional and transactional tasks while also influencing strategic issues. Many firms may need to alter their HR skills to be able to supply line managers with data and advice in order to execute these various jobs and become strategic partners.

Summing Up

For the development of adaptive leadership a new leadership development framework is required. Employees have a say in where they work, shaping the dialogue, shaping the workplace, and eventually impacting leadership choices, which is a key part of adaptable workplaces. Employees' well-being, passion for the job, and dedication to the firm are all enhanced when they have a sense of choice and control over when, how, and where they conduct their work. Adaptive ability will continue to determine who emerges on top and who goes away in 2022. HR executives can assist corporate leaders in evaluating their default habits and embracing their ability to adjust. HR analytics benefits firms by assisting them in making proactive decisions that help them mitigate risks and stay on top of things. It may assist in the provision of vital data and the subsequent improvement of spending, productivity, and operations, all of which benefit a business holistically. If you think this is an adaptive difficulty, you should spend some time investigating what's going on. You might enlist the help of your HR department or engage an outside expert to do an objective evaluation of what is pushing your staff to go.

CHAPTER NINE

INNOVATION ORIENTATION

Innovative Organizations Are More Adaptable To Their Surroundings And Outperform Their Competitors

"Success today requires the agility and drive to constantly rethink, reinvigorate, react, and reinvent." – Bill Gates

Organizations are incorporating sophisticated computer technologies into their organizational processes to enhance efficiency and improve service delivery thanks to the emergence of big data. However, the importance of analytics and big data in innovation within and between enterprises is at the center of this discussion. Most firms assimilate technology innovation through a complicated, haphazard, top-down approach. A constant and spontaneous adaption process, on the other hand, may be more natural and increase assimilation quality. It investigates the link between organizational structures and innovation, focusing on a variety of organizational design ideas. It also examines organizational innovation from the micro-level of organizational learning and knowledge generation. It claims that various organizational structures have distinct learning and knowledge patterns. It claims that organizations of various structural forms have varied learning and knowledge generation patterns, resulting in different sorts of inventive capacities. The debate then focuses to organizational adaptation and transformation, with an emphasis on whether and how companies can overcome inertia in the face of discontinuous technology developments and extreme adjustments in environmental conditions. For many businesses, innovation is a critical source of growth and a significant determinant of competitive advantage. To achieve innovation, many diverse actors must work together, and activities must be integrated across expert roles, knowledge domains, and application contexts. As a result, organizational formation is critical to the innovation process.

"Innovation separates between a leader and a follower," -Steve Jobs

The ability of a company to innovate is a prerequisite for the effective use of innovative resources and new technology. On the other hand, the introduction of new technology frequently confronts businesses with significant possibilities and problems, resulting in changes in management practices and the formation of new organizational structures. Organizational and technical advancements are inextricably linked.

Successful vs Unsuccessful

Why Do Adaptive Companies Have An Advantage In The Digital Age?

More organizations are seeking methods to brainstorm and cooperate smoothly this year, thanks to the advent of hybrid work. Miro is an online whiteboard application for teams that now lets 1,000 people collaborate on a board at the same time, owing to a 2021 technical upgrade. The software integrates with Teams, Zoom, Google Workspace, and others and includes a template gallery where established businesses (such as TED and Atlassian) may exchange example presentations, icebreaker ideas, and event-planning papers with other users. More than 400 of these have been added to what the business has nicknamed the Miroverse as of late autumn. These efforts to be more vital have helped Miro dramatically grow both its customer and user base.Miro increased from 20,000 to 130,000 paid clients between April 2020 and

January 2022. It collaborates with 99 percent of the world's top 100 corporations.

"The greatest approach to inspiring invention is to foster a culture of thanks and appreciation."- Anonymous

The site of employment Indeed, it responded to the Great Resignation by launching a number of new products aimed towards workers searching for new opportunities, including a new hiring platform in March 2021. The platform manages the whole process, automating some of the most time-consuming (and inconvenient) aspects of the recruiting and screening process, such as organizing job interviews—and then holding those interviews using its own videoconferencing module. Indeed serves job seekers in more than 60 countries and also provides various services targeted at making job seekers stand out, such as a résumé review service and a free wage transparency tool that allows workers to evaluate how their current compensation compares to that of their peers. Millions of job seekers have arranged interviews, which usually happen within a few days, and over 1 million people have had their résumés assessed. Indeed, a branch of Recruit Holdings, does not publish out its own financials, but Recruit recorded a 27.5 percent increase in sales and an almost 133 percent increase in operating profits in the nine months between March and December 2021. Competition for talent boosted the company's expansion, according to its financial records.

Many businesses went remote during the worst of the epidemic and have since resorted to a hybrid structure or have brought staff back full-time without much thought. Dropbox, which owns DocSend and HelloSign, wants to be more deliberate in its approach. Dropbox reimagined its offices as *"Dropbox Studios"* in July, with gathering areas geared for cross-team collaboration and team development rather than everyday work, after announcing its intention to go *"virtual first"* in October 2020. During the workday, the firm implemented four-hour *"Core Collaboration Hours,"* allowing workers to work flexibly outside of these windows for improved work-life integration. Dropbox had a strong financial quarter following the shift, with a double-digit revenue increase compared to the previous quarter.

Dialpad, the device-agnostic cloud communications platform, had a strong year in 2021, thanks to the debut of its videoconferencing product, Dialpad Meetings, and text and voice collaboration tool, Dialpad Channels. The company's voice intelligence solution, codenamed Vi, employs AI to assist employees with preserving meeting takeaways or addressing issues that arise during, say, contact between a client and a customer support person. Dialpad, which was founded by a number of former Google Voice employees, now aspires to be the only communications tool a company needs, whether for videoconferencing, audio conversations, or internal messaging. Hundreds of companies use the software-as-a-service concept to access the company's communications tools. Hundreds of firms aiming to streamline and simplify in a remote-first world use the privately held company's communications capabilities via a software-as-a-service approach. Among its publicly traded enterprise customers are Classpass, PagerDuty, ServiceFirst, TED, and Toast.

Who didn't have a Yellow Pages copy next to the phone? The legendary journal was once a lifeline for families all around the United Kingdom. For more than 50 years, the telephone directory has provided clients with business names, phone numbers, and addresses. Given the fast rise of digital and social media, CEO Richard Hanscott declared in 2017 that the firm would discontinue printing in 2019 and transition to digitising its entire operation. Since the company's inception in 1966, Hanscott has changed the business strategy while maintaining the integrity of the Yellow Pages by offering the same service to clients. It may feel strange not to possess a physical copy, but Yell.com offers the same service, just faster and better.

Today, Disney is one of the world's greatest media giants, yet it all started with humble origins. Since 1923, Disney has been capturing the imaginations of youngsters and families alike since

1923. Keeping a captivated audience, on the other hand, is no simple task. When the popularity of cult classics such as Donald Duck and Mickey Mouse began to wane, Disney reinvented itself time and again. Take, for example, the latest surge of live-action films that are bringing old favorites like Beauty and the Beast, The Jungle Book, and the much-anticipated Aladdin back to life.Disney's ability to adapt and change with the times while remaining true to its beginnings as a maker of timeless, iconic characters has been critical to its success. To stay relevant, Disney has bought Pixar Studios (in 2006 for $7.4 billion), Marvel (in 2009 for $6 billion), Star Wars (Lucasfilm in 2012 for $4 billion), and practically all of 21st Century Fox (external link) for $52 billion in shares.

Who could have predicted that Jeff Bezos' concept for an online bookshop, which he launched in his basement in Seattle in 1994, would become the world's largest internet retailer? Amazon has taken the globe by storm, and it all began with a product advertised as "the world's largest book shop." Since then, the internet behemoth has irreversibly altered our consumption habits. Is it possible to get fresh meals via the internet? Done. Same-day or even same-hour delivery? Absolutely.

Amazon has redefined convenience and will continue to do so - Bezos sends out the identical 1997 Annual Report Letter to Shareholders, emphasizing a constant focus on 'obsessing over consumers' and a determination to make daring rather than cautious decisions. The Swedish startup, which was founded in 2008, has revolutionized the way music is delivered and enjoyed in an amazingly short amount of time. Spotify's streaming service, which has 70 million subscribers, has done the unthinkable: it has gotten people to pay for music again. Global revenues soared last year to an estimated $10.8bn, but with Spotify paying out a huge portion of its revenue to the music industry, largely in royalties, how will it move forward without losing money?

Last year's global sales surged to an estimated $10.8 billion, but how can Spotify continue to make money if it pays a major portion of its earnings to the music business, mostly in royalties? Could

Spotify be on the verge of disrupting the music industry once more, following in the footsteps of Netflix? Could it try to start its own music label to develop original content rather than pay fees for record rights?

Kodak was formerly the most well-known and groundbreaking name in the world of photography and filmmaking. The firm was instrumental in the development of cameras that were portable, inexpensive, transportable, and eventually affordable for the average person. However, with the development of the digital camera in 1975, Kodak failed to react to technological changes. Remember when anything was referred to as a *"Kodak moment"*? Kodak controlled the photographic business and was once associated with snapping a picture.However, the firm filed for bankruptcy in 2013 because of its failure to adapt quickly enough to the introduction of digital photography, which rendered camera film useless for all but the most ardent traditionalists. Could it, however, be resurrected now? Kodak's stock price on the New York Stock Exchange more than quadrupled in January. The increase followed Kodak's announcement that it would establish its own cryptocurrency, KodakCoin. KodakCoin is a cryptocurrency aimed at photographers that is part of a larger blockchain ecosystem dedicated to safeguarding photographers and giving them control over their image rights. Could Kodak demonstrate that the *"Kodak moment"* can be resurrected by taking a proactive approach to new technology? The organization has always held the notion that a printed picture will continue to be valued and appreciated by clients above a digital image. Of course, they were mistaken, but it was too late to recover their losses by the time they stopped selling classic film cameras in 2004. Since declaring bankruptcy in 2012, Kodak has been striving to reinvent itself. In an unusual turn of events, the business secured a $765 million federal loan in 2020 from the Trump administration to create 25% of the active components for generic pharmaceuticals in the US.

So, what can other companies learn from these fearless innovators? If it ain't broke, don't fix it.

When you're done altering, you're done. Maybe it's just a matter of not being too attached to the past. Google is largely regarded as one of the world's most agile and inventive businesses. That isn't to say it hasn't had its share of big-company organizational problems. The alphabet, for example, was created by it. When it put its well-established companies (Google, Gmail, YouTube, Android, and Maps) with Google and its more speculative businesses (Calico, Waymo, Nest, Google Fiber, GV, and CapitalG) with Alphabet, the corporation set out to compete more effectively in the face of continual change.

The goal was to isolate the company's more established money earners from its expansion plans. The new structure would offer each company the freedom to make decisions based on the specifics of its market while avoiding the resource fights that stymie other huge technological firms. Google established a more flexible organization that could act depending on the imperatives of each individual business rather than forcing strategic judgments about where to play in a static, function-driven organization and team structure. An adaptable company has this mindset—namely, the ability to apply inner-game agility to operations, planning, and people management.

Take chances and prioritize new ideas by allowing teams to handle challenges together and giving them full ownership of choices; and focus the right people on the right objectives using qualitative and quantitative tools instead of waiting for annual planning sessions. Strategic planning methods that are unable to adjust rapidly enough to market developments and the actions of competitors might have unfavorable outcomes. Consider Microsoft's smartphone experience. It's hard to believe now, but prior to 2007, Windows Mobile 6 was the mobile market leader, with a 30% share over Palm, BlackBerry, and Symbian.

However, once the iPhone and Android were released, the game was over. Despite its historic purchase of Nokia's phone company, Microsoft has slowly lost market share since then and is now a tiny player in what is perhaps the most significant area of technology.

Too many businesses maintain their holy cows, allocating and allocating resources to the same priority year after year in order to ensure that everyone receives their 2% to 3% raise. Instead of sticking to the financial calendar, the most effective leadership teams can unleash funds and resources to put behind crucial new projects when strategic needs change. Amazon's acquisition of Whole Foods threw the retail industry's assumptions into disarray. Grocers have long thought that the food industry is immune to disruption, which has led to a delay in investing in omnichannel solutions. They're now in danger of being swallowed up by Amazon's innovation engine, which spends $16 billion a year (almost 12% of sales) on *technology and content,* with much of it going to IT-related R&D. According to Gartner, retail and wholesale organizations spend significantly less on IT than retail and wholesale organizations, spending only about 1.5 percent of sales on IT. Too many businesses either underinvest in innovative ideas or abandon them too soon. The most adaptable businesses recognize and develop their own innovations and disruption prospects. They invest for the long term by investing in a methodical manner.They take the long view by investing methodically in ideas that may not produce fruit for years (or ever), but when they do, the results might be extremely disruptive. Creating self-organizing teams Digital efforts generally span numerous departments within a company, and they are unlikely to succeed if departmental barriers get in the way. Many cross-functional SWAT teams with decentralized decision-making and the authority to make quick, day-to-day choices inside their group are needed by companies.

When a company is forced to modify or adapt, it can prosper. Take the bull by the horns and lead the market towards the next iPhone or Google. However, some people are unaware that in order to be successful, they must welcome change. It's critical to acquire some crucial business skills, whether you own a firm or work in a department where you're responsible for a particular amount of duty and accountability. You provide a variety of online and virtual classroom training courses to assist you in filling up any gaps. Before you get started, if you're thinking about changing careers, You've put together a list of resources for you:They may have failed to adapt, but that does not imply they are no longer in business. Keep an eye out to see whether any of the ones you recall are still in operation today.

Blockbuster is a company that rents out movies and video games. At its peak, Blockbuster had over 9,000 locations worldwide and employed 84,000 people.They were head and shoulders above most other rental outlets in terms of the number and range of titles. Blockbuster's economic model needed to evolve in response to the emergence of Netflix and on-demand streaming, but it did not. Blockbuster did not adapt to the times by adopting a trend that would eventually lead to its demise. Jonathan Salem Baskin, a former marketing communications executive, claimed that digital would have transformed Blockbuster's business for sure.

After the merger of Houston Natural Gas and InterNorth, Enron was formed as an American energy, commodities, and service corporation. Enron had 20,000 employees and was one of the world's largest energy, natural gas, and communications corporations. For the sixth year in a row, Fortune magazine named it America's most innovative corporation. Enron's collapse occurred after a scandal showed that the business was plagued with fraud and wrongdoing. To hide dishonesty in their accounting information, they employed a range of misleading and fraudulent accounting methods and strategies. They were essentially misrepresenting any expected or possible earnings from any asset as reality when they weren't (more can be read on that here).

There were once 80 million Blackberry users around the world, including former US President Barack Obama, who stopped using his in 2016.In the mid-to late-2000s, Blackberry Messenger was the dominant form of professional and personal contact, with everyone demanding to know your pin. In a nutshell, the iPhone is doomed. Apple began to dominate the mobile industry by supporting Bring Your Own Device (BYOD) rules and guidelines within organizations, whereas Blackberry disregarded touch-screen-based technologies. In 2014, three years after Apple had incorporated Siri into all of their devices, there were rumors that Blackberry was working on a Siri-like voice assistant named Blackberry Assistant. Blackberry's failure to innovate resulted in their demise.

Because of their inability to innovate, Blackberry quickly fell to a 0.2 percent market share by early 2016. Kodak was the market leader in photographic film during the twentieth century, having been founded in 1888. They came up with the *"Kodak moment"* phrase, which was used everywhere, and they even got a shout-out from Pitbull in his single *"Give Me Everything."* Kodak's demise was due to their fear of innovation. They built the first digital camera in 1975, but abandoned it owing to concerns that it would suffocate their photographic film juggernaut. After that, digital seized over, and Kodak's competitors, notably Fuji, outlasted the erstwhile photo monarchs. In 2012, Kodak declared bankruptcy, then resurfaced in 2013, substantially smaller and focused on business clients.

Facebook entered the arena with a superior user experience and the capacity to connect people via more than simply music, which is what MySpace essentially became as bands and musicians uploaded their songs and mixtapes nonstop. Through Facebook, users were able to connect with current and former friends who had the same hobbies and interests.

Yahoo was founded in 1994 and immediately rose to prominence as the go-to site for email, news, and online searches. The downfall of the corporation was caused by a series of poor business decisions. For example, Yahoo missed out on a $1 billion deal to purchase Google in 2002, and then a $1.1 billion deal to buy Facebook in 2006. Yahoo has also been chastised for mismanaging Flickr and Tumblr, failing to prioritize the hiring of high-calibre programming talent, and a leadership team that lacks direction. Yahoo was sold to Verizon in 2016 for just $4.8 billion after a number of failures. In comparison, at its height in 2000, the corporation was valued at $125 billion. Yahoo was the most-read news and media website in 2016, with over 7 billion monthly views, making it the world's sixth most visited website. They controlled 21% of the internet advertising industry in 2005, indicating that they were the market leaders. In 2011, Yahoo's email service had 281 million subscribers, making it the world's third-largest provider of web-based email services.

Their demise was due to poor management of their expansion. They were already number one, but in order to achieve their goal of becoming an internet gateway, they decided to outsource their search engine to Microsoft Bing. When Yahoo had the opportunity to purchase Google for $5 billion in 2002, they turned it down. In 2006, Yahoo had a contract to acquire Facebook for $1 billion, but the offer was lowered, prompting Mark Zuckerberg to pull out. As of March 22, 2018, Facebook's stock price was $163 billion. Yahoo is currently ranked fourth among the largest internet marketers, a position they are fighting to keep.

Look at this, another camera supplier. In 1991, Polaroid's instant film and cameras helped the company reach a sales record of $3 billion. They possessed the patent on their instant photography method, making them the most well-known names associated with the procedure, which they are still referred to today. Organizations that are unable or unwilling to adapt to disruption, technology improvements, and changing consumer needs have been demonstrated time and time again to fail in the long run. Seven businesses have learnt this lesson the hard way.

Nokia was previously recognized for being incredibly adaptable and forward-thinking, so its downfall was unexpected. In 1996, the business made a significant investment in research and development and created the first smartphone. Nokia, on the other hand, failed to see the importance of software, especially applications, and miscalculated the quick move to smartphones in the years that followed. Nokia, for example, made more than half of its revenue in 2007.

Nokia, for example, made more than half of all earnings in the mobile phone market in 2007, yet the majority of those revenues did not come from smartphones. Apple, on the other hand, was devoting equal attention to both hardware and software development and was well ahead of the curve when it came to smartphone advances. Nokia had only 3% of the worldwide smartphone market by 2013, and it sold its handset division to Microsoft for $7.2 billion in August of that year. Another camera company has gone out of business because they underestimated the impact that digital cameras would have. Polaroid Corporation went bankrupt in 2001, just a decade after earning its highest-ever single-year revenue.

Xerox established the Xerox Palo Alto Research Center (also known as Xerox PARC) in 1970 to explore future technologies. Laser printers, Ethernet, and a forerunner to the modern PC were all developed at the Xerox PARC. However, despite investing substantially in research and development and producing several groundbreaking technologies, the firm struggled to capitalize on market potential and achieve commercial success, ultimately losing out to a corporation with a stronger brand and a far larger ambition. In 1958, Xerox introduced the Xerox 914 photocopier, which revolutionized document printing. It is widely regarded as the most successful single product in history, generating $60 million in sales for Xerox in only three years and rising to nearly $500 million by 1965. Despite having invented the graphical user interface (GUI) and a commercial version of the mouse, when the Macintosh computer was released in 1984, it was Steve Jobs and Apple that realized the benefits of these technologies. Xerox was ultimately unable to capitalize on its ideas and inventions in order to operate a viable, commercial corporation.

Xerox's dilemma was that their own inventions were spurned by their own directors, which led to its demise. Xerox researchers and engineers pioneered a number of aspects of personal computing, but the company's board of directors ordered the engineers to share their discoveries with Apple personnel.These innovations were later taken by Apple and Microsoft, who went on to become the two most powerful computing companies, leaving Xerox in the dust.

Summing Up

A constant and spontaneous adaption process may be more natural and increase assimilation quality. It investigates the link between organizational structures and innovation, focusing on a variety of organizational design ideas. The ability of a company to innovate is a prerequisite for the effective use of innovative resources and new technology. Many businesses went remote during the worst of the epidemic and have since resorted to a hybrid structure or have brought staff back full-time without much thought.When a company is forced to modify or adapt, it can prosper. Take the bull by the horns and lead the market towards the next iPhone or Google.

Conclusion

Organizations That Excel In Adaptability Foster Employees' Creativity

"You can't build an adaptable organization without adaptable people - and individuals change only when they have to, or when they want to." -Anonymous

- Adaptability is a feature that can lead to the development of other desirable attributes in people and organizations. A company that can function effectively in unforeseen conditions can adopt whole new approaches. Such businesses have the technology, manpower, and tools to outperform the competition at any moment. Adaptive organizations are better suited to lead and set the pace for a whole industry.
- Long-term success requires adaptability. It is critical to survive in times like today, when the world is in the grip of a worldwide epidemic. Because they failed to adapt to the ever-changing business landscape, company giants such as Myspace, Kodak, and RadioShack are now just memories. Everything in an organization is influenced by culture. It's just the way things are done here. A culture that encourages individuals to feel psychologically good while also motivating them to achieve peak performance motivates them to be extremely successful. As a consequence, dedication, trust, motivation, kinship, focus, and social involvement characterize the organization and workforce. These are the characteristics and behaviors that make businesses so successful.
- Because capability building is a natural function of an organization, the goal of leadership is to guide it toward an enabling mission, which leads to vision. For example, Jeff Bezos is well-known for his belief that meetings centred on

PowerPoint did not result in increased capability to carry out their mission. As a consequence, he came up with the narrative meeting process. You must be intentional and vocal about the importance of learning in your organization, and you must welcome input from individuals, groups, and the entire organization. This enables your mental models to be constantly updated to reflect reality, making your organization adaptive, agile, and responsive to both internal and external conditions and events of consequence, increasing your likelihood of market dominance and success significantly more than your competition.

- Leaders must always provide coherence to a continuous improvement process by buffering it from—or linking it to—other imperatives that exist in a district at any given time if it is to thrive. Leaders will encounter conflicting expectations without any buffering or bridging, making it impossible to produce anything cohesive.

- When the whole organization supports these cultural norms and practices, the power of adaptation develops. You've discovered a few key factors based on your expertise with both virtual and in-person capability development. Organizations must grab the chance to mix these components with the more conventional in-person immersion experience as they enter a new chapter of hybrid work.

- In actuality, only a small number of leaders are prepared to listen to others who disagree with them. What such leaders fail to realize is that listening does not always imply forsaking one's own objectives. It simply implies that you have a better understanding of your employees' requirements. As a result, you'll be able to work more efficiently to implement modifications.

- Although adaptive leadership demands a significant amount of work, it pays off handsomely. Adaptive businesses, according to trustworthy statistics, reap enormous financial and operational benefits. Even during moments of turbulence, they are able to withstand storms and surge to the top. Providing enough time and space for the job helps instructors stay motivated and not feel overwhelmed. Building a culture of relational trust allows employees to use the change effort's procedures and structures in ways that are more about learning than performance, and to have open and honest discussions that lead to better practice.

- For the development of adaptive leadership a new leadership development framework is required. One that can be given at scale and creates adaptable leaders at all levels, sooner in their careers and in the flow of their work. The new model stresses learning in the context of the organization's business conditions, processes, and objectives, as well as quick implementation of what has been learned. Starting with helping leaders understand the business, including its goals, mission, and goods and services, there are multiple activities and numerous keys to producing adaptable leaders. HR executives must rethink workforce and employee planning, management, performance, and experience methods as the pandemic resets important work patterns.

- Hierarchies must play a supporting role in enabling a constantly evolving network of teams. These groups require adaptable leaders. Leaders who are flexible the way people live, work, and conduct business will continue to be shaped and reshaped by long-term upheaval and change. Adaptive firms must look beyond incremental development and address current practices' flaws on a regular basis. Adaptive leaders need to climb up on the roof from time to time to observe what's coming over the horizon. When they detect the potential for disruption, they must move rapidly to plan responses in concert with other leaders.

- Employers must implement flexible work arrangements to enable current living choices, according to younger generations. This applies to both when and where to work. Flexible work environments have also been a major success factor in several firms for attracting female professionals and balancing inequity, with enhanced workplace safety and health records as a side effect. Despite this, most firms see flexible work environments as a possibility, a fantasy, reserved for the rare Friday-at-home rather than the norm. In a turbulent, unpredictable, complicated, and ambiguous environment, a players defined in practice through an iterative, incremental, and emergent delivery strategy becomes a valuable survival weapon.

- Remember that self-organized systems can evolve and enhance their behavior and structure in order to better adapt to changing external situations. Predicting trends over the next day, month, quarter, or year is also difficult. Following a meeting with your finance staff, shareholders, and vendors, and with a comprehensive understanding of the company's financial state—including current cash flow, credit situation, income and costs, and so on adapting to change is what makes you useful, relevant, and on the cutting edge of innovation. Failure, learning, accountability, and change are all things that an adaptive company embraces. Adaptive firms strive to provide proactive innovation, satisfy consumers and other stakeholders, and lead with appreciation and wisdom in the corporate environment.

About The Author

Dr. Amit is the founder of Accumentor India, a consultancy firm set up by him in the human resource solution space, which is focused on developing processes for people. It offers consultancy in learning management, mentorship, performance coaching, training and development, psychometric analysis, HR processes and interventions. He was formerly the Director of Expertell Learning Point.

Dr. Amit Das is an experienced sales, training, and learning professional with more than 20 years of working history in the healthcare, medical devices, and learning management industries. Dr. Amit is a seasoned training & learning professional with rich experience and a successful track record in aligning learning and training solutions to key business strategy with a strong focus on flawless execution excellence to facilitate individual, business divisional, and organisational performance. He keeps relentless focus on measuring training impact and ROI, people capability building graphs, training process governance, performance coaching, and strategic thinking. These have been some of his key individual success traits. His core capabilities include performance coaching, designing training and development frameworks and facilitation of technical skill building, psychometric assessment and analysis, competency framework development and assessments, content design and facilitation of soft skills and leadership programmes, E-Learning Platform development, Learning Management Systems, Learning Impact Measurement, Talent Analysis and Performance Management System Review, Performance Coaching and Counselling.

His interests are in the areas of leadership development, coaching competency, mentorship, and motivational complexities related to organizational issues. His hobbies include public speaking, content creation, and reading books.

He has a Ph.D. and a Fellowship in strategic learning, along with his first class degrees in Human Resource Management and Corporate Laws from the top business schools in India. He is a certified professional coach from U.K. and behavioral coach from U.S.A.

References

- *Leadership: Theory and practice. Los Angeles, CA: SAGE Publications, Inc by Northouse, P. published 2019*
- *All Systems Go: The Change Imperative for Whole System Reform (Paperback)by Michael Fullan, published 2010*
- *The Constructivist Leader (Paperback) by Deborah Walker,published 1995*
- *Credibility: How Leaders Gain and Lose It, Why People Demand It (Paperback) by James M. Kouzes, published 1993*
- *Appreciative Leadership: Focus on What Works to Drive Winning Performance and Build a Thriving Organization (Hardcover) by Diana Whitney, published 2010*
- *Thinking, Fast and Slow (Hardcover) by Daniel Kahneman, published 2011*
- *The Checklist Manifesto: How to Get Things Right (Hardcover) by Atul Gawande, published 2009*
- *The Heart of Change: Real-Life Stories of How People Change Their Organizations (Hardcover) by John P. Kotter (Goodreads Author), published 2002*
- *Harvard Business Review on Leading Through Change (Paperback) by Harvard Business School Press (Compilation), published 2006*
- *Boards That Lead: When to Take Charge, When to Partner, and When to Stay Out of the Way (Hardcover) by Ram Charan, published 2013*
- *Innovation in the Schoolhouse: Entrepreneurial Leadership in Education (ebook)by Jack Leonard, published 2013*
- *Chaos, Complexity and Leadership 2012 (Hardcover) by Santo Banerjee (Editor), published 2013*
- *Checklist for Change: Making American Higher Education a Sustainable Enterprise (Hardcover)by Robert Zemsky, published 2013*
- *Nudge: Improving Decisions About Health, Wealth, and Happiness*

(Paperback) by Richard H. Thaler, published 2008
- *Leverage Leadership: A Practical Guide to Building Exceptional Schools (Paperback) by Doug Lemov, published 2012*
- *Rethinking Leadership: A Collection of Articles (Paperback) by Thomas J. Sergiovanni (Editor), published 1999*
- *Leadership on the Line, With a New Preface: Staying Alive Through the Dangers of Change (Kindle Edition) by Ronald A. Heifetz*
- *We Want to Do More Than Survive: Abolitionist Teaching and the Pursuit of Educational Freedom (Hardcover) by Bettina L. Love, published 2019*
- *Solving Tough Problems: An Open Way of Talking, Listening, and Creating New Realities (Hardcover) by Adam Kahane (Goodreads Author), published 2004*
- *Change the World: How Ordinary People Can Accomplish Extraordinary Things (Hardcover) by Robert E. Quinn (Goodreads Author), published 2000*
- *Practical Approaches to Marketing Analytics in the Digital Age (ebook) by Cesar A. Brea, published 2012*
- *The Innovative University: Changing the DNA of Higher Education from the Inside Out (Hardcover)by Clayton M. Christensen, published 2011*
- *Reinventing Higher Education: The Promise of Innovation (Hardcover) by Ben Wildavsky (Editor), published 2011*
- *Bass & Stogdill's Handbook of Leadership: Theory, Research & Managerial Applications (Hardcover) by Bernard M. Bass, published 1990*
- *The practice of Adaptive Leadership: Tools and Tactics for Changing Your Organization and the world (Hardcover) by Ronald A. Heifetz, published 2009*
- *The Third Side: Why We Fight and How We Can Stop (Paperback) by William Ury, published 2000*
- *Accelerate: Building Strategic Agility for a Faster-Moving World (Hardcover) by John P. Kotter (Goodreads Author), published 2012*
- *How Colleges Change: Understanding, Leading, and Enacting Change (ebook) by Adrianna Kezar, published 2013*

REFERENCES

- *Adaptation Studies and Learning: New Frontiers (Paperback) by Laurence Raw, published 2013*
- *More Than 50 Ways to Build Team Consensus (Paperback) by R. Bruce Williams, published 1993*
- *Adaptability: Responding Effectively to Change (Paperback) by Allan Calarco, published 2006*
- *Building Resiliency: How to Thrive in Times of Change (Paperback) by Mary Lynn Pulley, published 2001*
- *Playing to Win: How Strategy Really Works (Hardcover) by A.G. Lafley, published 2013*
- *Leadership Without Easy Answers (Hardcover) by Ronald A. Heifetz, published 1994*
- *Influencer: The Power to Change Anything (Hardcover) by Kerry Patterson, published 2007*
- *Leadership on the Line: Staying Alive Through the Dangers of Leading (Hardcover)by Ronald A. Heifetz , published 2002*
- *Leading for Powerful Learning: A Guide for Instructional Leaders (Paperback) by Angela Breidenstein, published 2012*
- *Theory U: Leading from the Future as it Emerges (Hardcover) by C. Otto Scharmer (Goodreads Author), published 2007*
- *Complex Adaptive Leadership: Embracing Paradox and Uncertainty (Hardcover) by Nick Obolensky, published 2000*
- *Invaluable Master the 10 Skills You Need to Skyrocket Your Career by Maya Grossman, published 2020|*
- *Invaluable, Master the 10 Skills You Need to Skyrocket Your Career by Maya Grossman, published 2020*
- *The Effective Executive , The Definitive Guide to Getting the Right Things Done by Peter F. Drucker, Zachary First, Jim Collins, publish 2017*
- *The Leadership Challenge, How to Make Extraordinary Things Happen in Organizations by James M. Kouzes, Barry Z. Posner, published 2017*
- *Multipliers, How the Best Leaders Make Everyone Smarter by Liz Wiseman, Greg McKeown, published 2014*

REFERENCES

- *The Leadership Gap, What Gets Between You and Your Greatness by Lolly Daskal, published 2017*
- *The Power of Positive Leadership, How and Why Positive Leaders Transform Teams and Organizations and Change the World by Jon Gordon, published 2017*
- *Wooden on Leadership, How to Create a Winning Organization by John Wooden, Steve Jamison, published 2005*
- *Learning Leadership, The Five Fundamentals of Becoming an Exemplary Leader by James M. Kouzes, Barry Z. Posner, published 2016*
- *5 Levels of Leadership, Proven Steps to Maximize Your Potential by John C. Maxwell, published 2013*
- *Real Leadership, 9 Simple Practices for Leading and Living with Purpose by John Addison, John David Mann, published|2016*
- *TouchPoints, Creating Powerful Leadership Connections in the Smallest of Moments by Douglas Conant, Mette Norgaard, published 2011*
- *Organizational Culture and Leadership by Edgar H. Schein, published 2010*
- *The Practice of Adaptive Leadership, Tools and Tactics for Changing Your Organization and the World by Ronald A. Heifetz, Marty Linsky, Alexander Grashow, published 2009*

9 798887 040899